Book 8
Advanced Repertoire

Succeeding with the Masters®
THE FESTIVAL COLLECTION®

Compiled and edited by HELEN MARLAIS

About the Series

Welcome to *The Festival Collection®*! This nine-volume series is designed to give students and teachers a great variety of fabulous repertoire from the Baroque, Classical, Romantic, and Twentieth/Twenty-First Centuries. The series is carefully leveled from elementary through advanced repertoire. These pieces are true crowd pleasers and will showcase students' technical and musical abilities. Each level covers the gamut of your repertoire needs, from works that showcase power and bravura, to pieces that develop a student's sense of control and finesse. Having a wide selection of works with pedagogically-correct leveling will help make your repertoire selections easier and your students' performances more successful.

Each book includes a CD recording of all of the corresponding works to guide students in their interpretation. The editing in the scores reflects these CD performances. While the CD performances are consistent with the editing in the books, and vice versa, they also demonstrate an appropriate degree of interpretive license. My goal is to instill an appreciation for accurate performances, while nurturing a sense for stylistically appropriate interpretive license. The preparatory level and books one through six were recorded by Helen Marlais, and books seven and eight were recorded by Helen Marlais, Chiu-Ling Lin, and Frances Renzi, giving students at these higher levels the opportunity to hear three different performance styles.

The Festival Collection® is a companion series to the *Succeeding with the Masters®* series. *Succeeding with the Masters®* provides the student with practice strategies and valuable information about the musical characteristics of each era. *The Festival Collection®* expands the repertoire selection with numerous additional top-drawer pedagogical works in a wide array of styles, and with different musical and technical demands. There is no duplication of repertoire between these two series. All of the pieces in both series are motivational and exciting for students to learn as well as for teachers to teach!

Enjoy the series!

Helen Marlais

THE F·J·H MUSIC COMPANY INC.
Frank J. Hackinson

Production: Frank J. Hackinson
Production Coordinators: Joyce Loke and Satish Bhakta
Cover Design and Art Direction: Gwen Terpstra, Terpstra Design, San Francisco, CA,
Cover Art Concept: Helen Marlais
Illustration: Keith Criss, TradigitalWorks, Oakland, CA
Engraving: Tempo Music Press, Inc.
Printer: Tempo Music Press, Inc.

ISBN-13: 978-1-56939-596-7

The Festival Collection® Book 8

The Festival Collection® Book 8

ALLEMANDE

from *French Suite No. 5, BWV 816*

Johann Sebastian Bach
(1685-1750)

Courante

from *French Suite No. 5*, BWV 816

Johann Sebastian Bach
(1685-1750)

17
f
20
23
cresc.
26
29
fp

Sonata
(K.87, L.33)

Domenico Scarlatti
(1685-1757)

p espressivo

SONATA

(K.25, L.481)

Domenico Scarlatti
(1685-1757)

N.B. Dynamic markings are editorial.

24
mf
28
L.H.
simile
32
36
f
mp
41

46
mf
50
mf
54
L.H.
L.H.
simile
58
mp
62
cresc.

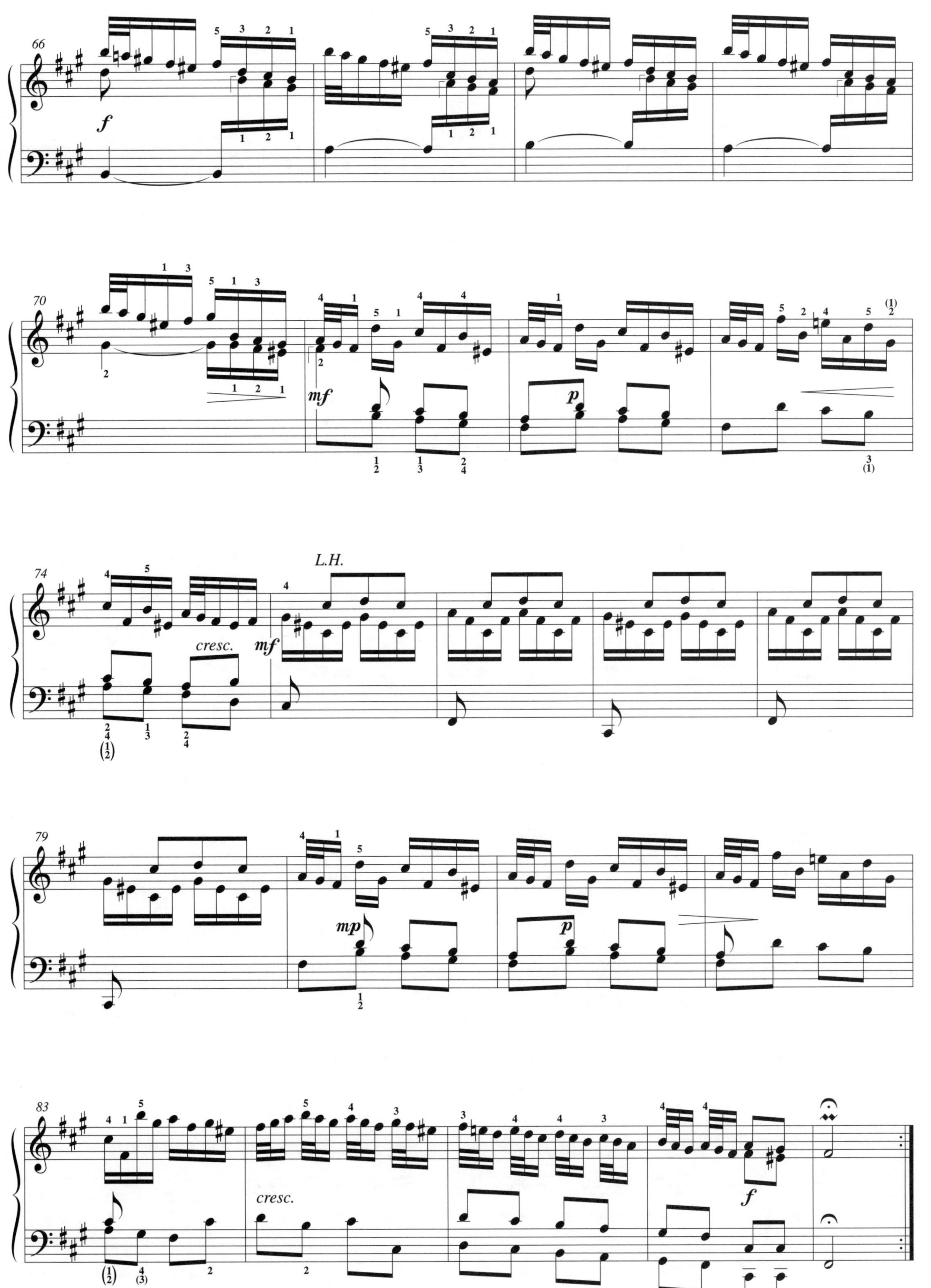
cresc.
L.H.
mf
mp
p
f
cresc.

Prelude and Fugue No. 2

from *The Well-Tempered Clavier, Book 1*, BWV 847

Johann Sebastian Bach
(1685-1750)

Praeludium II

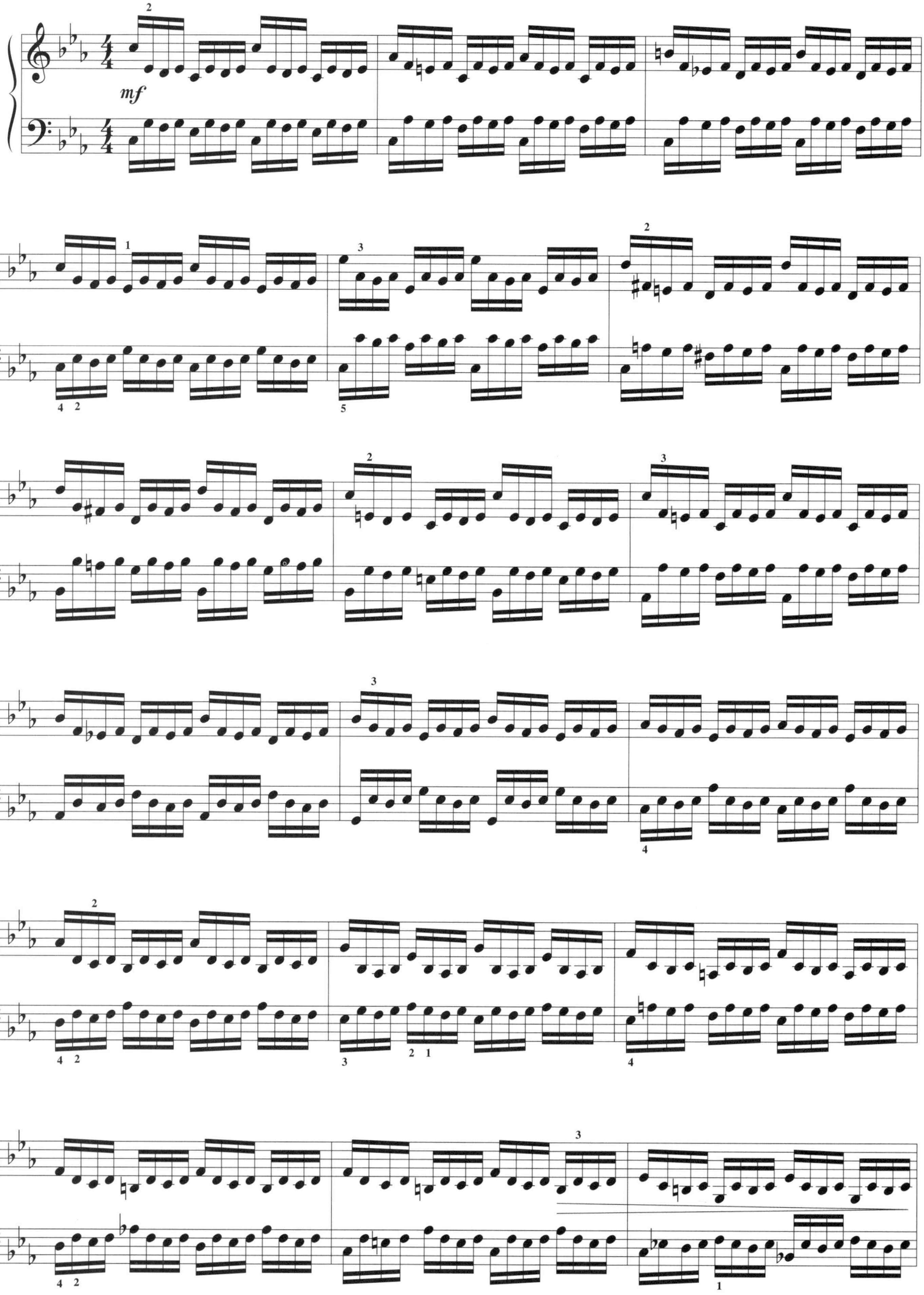

mp
cresc.
mf
Presto
Adagio
Allegro

Fuga II

mf
p
mf
p
mp
cresc.
mf
f

Prelude and Fugue No. 9

from *The Well-Tempered Clavier, Book 1*, BWV 854

Johann Sebastian Bach
(1685-1750)

Praeludium IX

mp
cresc.
mf

Fuga IX

cresc.
mf

Air with Variations

(The Harmonious Blacksmith)

from *Suite No. 5 in E Major, HWV 430*

George Frideric Handel
(1685-1759)

Double 2
mf
mp
p
tr
(tr)
a)

Double 3

Double 5

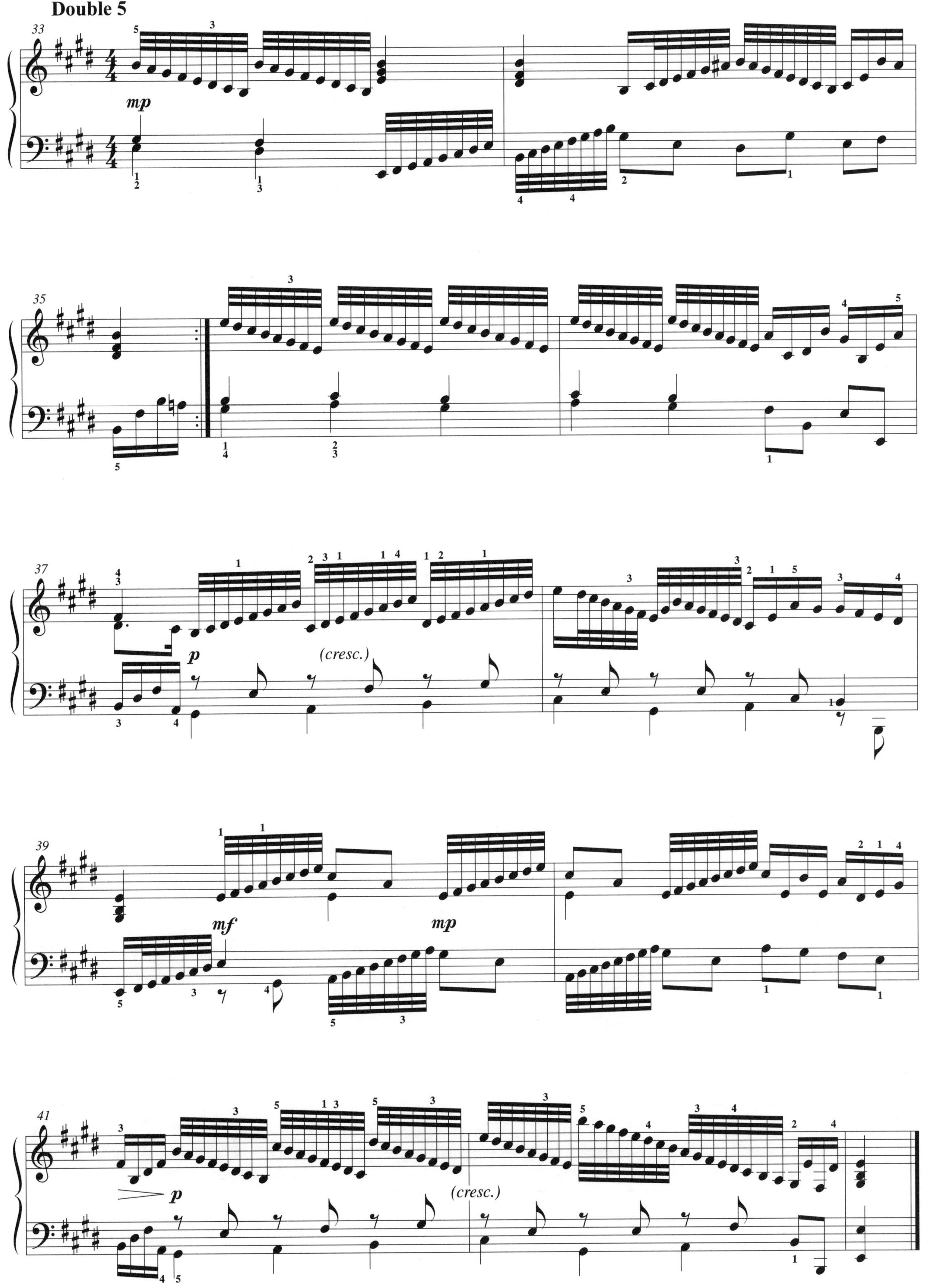

Dem Fürsten Nikolaus Esterházy gewidmet

Sonata in F Major

(No. 38, Hob. XVI/33)

Franz Joseph Haydn
(1732-1809)

First Movement

N.B. Dynamic markings are editorial.

cresc.
f
p
sfz
sfz
mf
p
mf
p
cresc.
f
tr
meno f
tr
cresc.
f

mp
c)
mf
sempre cresc.
f
p
cresc.
mf
c)

69
cresc.
ped. simile
72
74
p
76
f
fz
fz
79
mf
fz
81
fz
fz

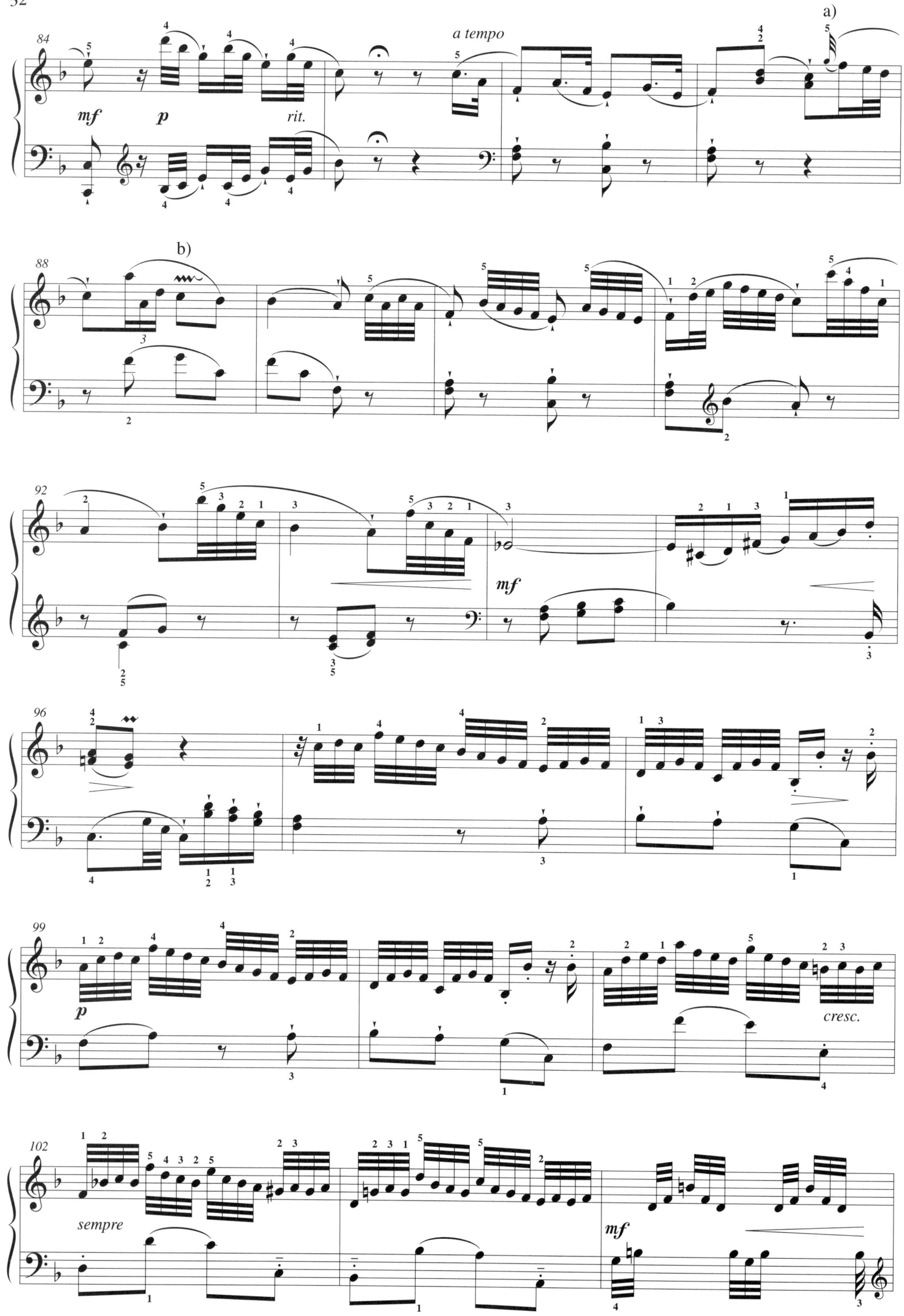
a tempo
a)
mf
p
rit.
b)
mf
mf
p
cresc.
sempre
mf

105
d)
tr
111
113
mp
mf
p
116
mf
p
119
cresc.
mf
f
122
tr
meno f
tr
125
cresc.
f
d)
etc.

Second Movement

mf
mp
p
mp
mf
p
cresc.
mf

pp
cresc.
mf
p
mp
cresc. sempre
mf
f
mp
b)
b)
etc.

mf
pp
mf
p
f
mp
mf
p
pp
rit.

Third Movement

p
pp
mp
f
p
cresc.
mf
mp
p
f
p
mf
f
p

legato
cresc.
mf
f
sempre f
mp
cresc.
mf
f
mf
p
cresc.
sempre cresc.
f

p
mf
f
p
pp
mp
cresc.

Dedicated to Prince Carl von Lichnowsky

SONATA IN C MINOR

Sonata Pathétique, Opus 13

First and Second Movements

Ludwig van Beethoven
(1770-1827)

First Movement

Grave

ped. simile

dim.

ped. simile

cresc.

Attacca subito il' allegro

Allegro molto e con brio
p
(p) cresc.
p
cresc.
p
sf
sf
sf
sf
p
cresc.
sf

42
47
L.H. under
53
60
67
74
rfz
rfz

81
decresc.
88
pp
p
93
cresc.
98
f
p
103
cresc.
108
f

113
p
117
cresc.
121
f
125
f
129
1.
2.
ff
ff

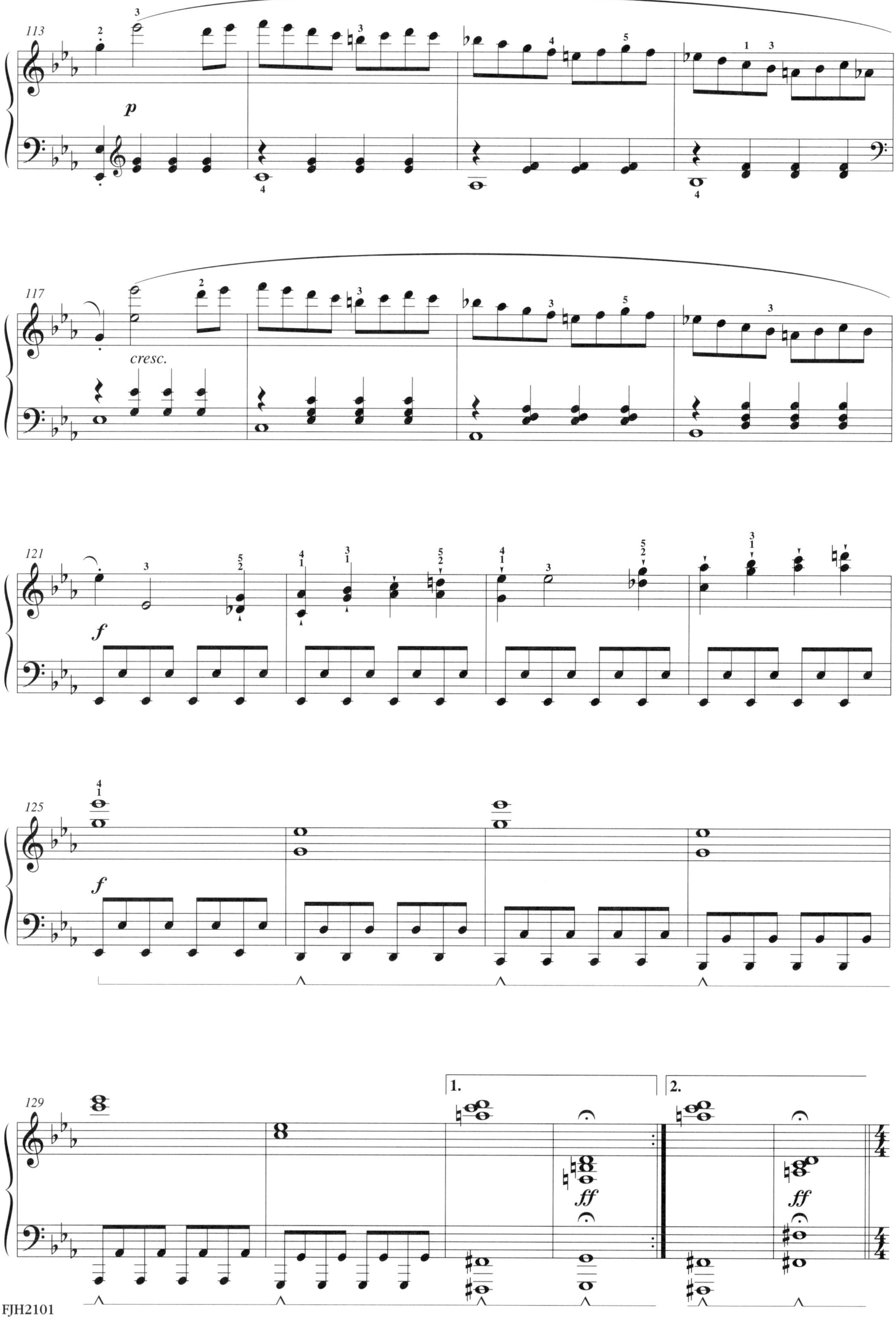

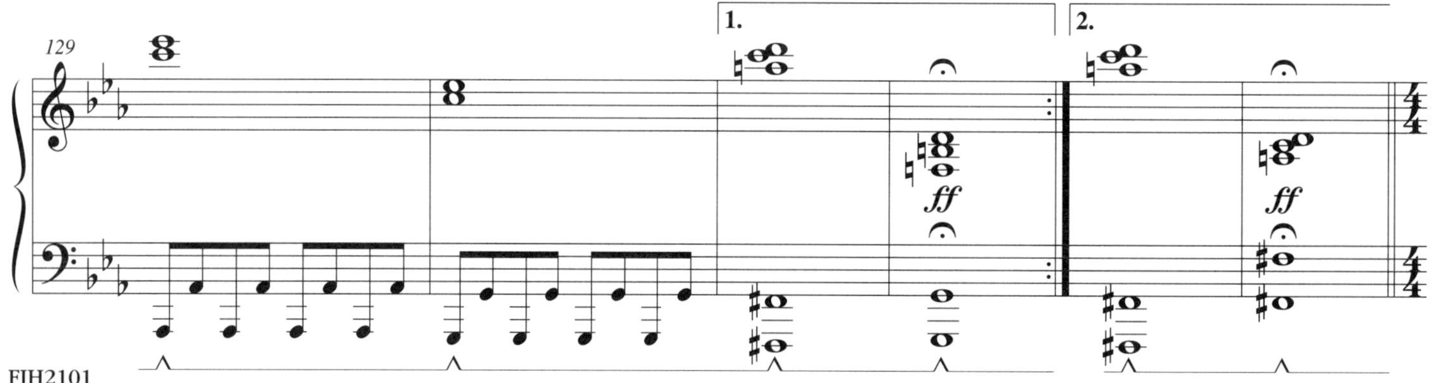

Tempo I
fp
fp
fp
p
decresc.
pp
Allegro molto e con brio
p cresc.
f
p
f
p
cresc.
p

166
pp
171
cresc.
175
sf
tr
pp
180
cresc.
sf
tr
185
sf
tr
sf
tr
189
fp

193
197
p
sf
cresc.
202
p
207
sf
cresc.
212
p
cresc.
217
p
cresc.
p

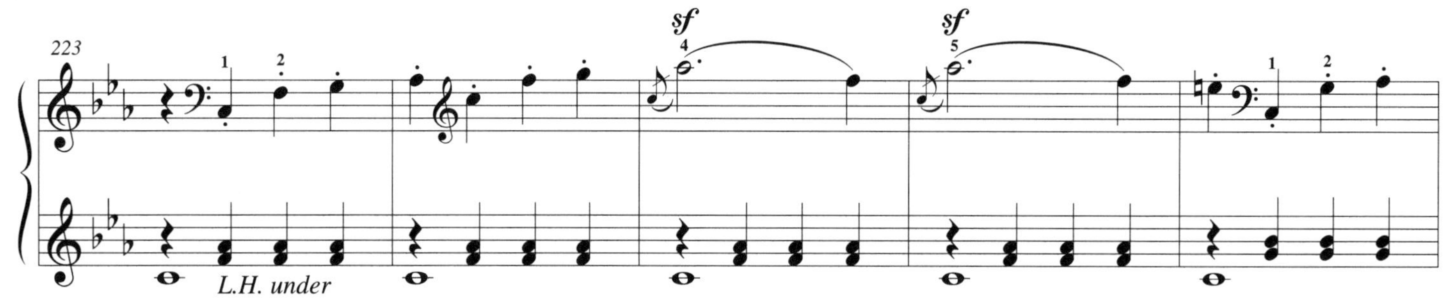
223
sf
sf
L.H. under

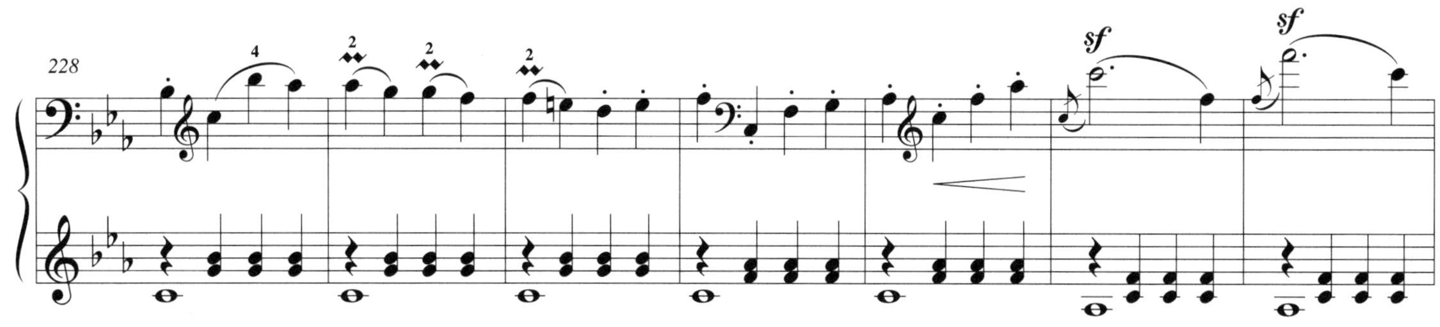
228
sf
sf

235
p
sf

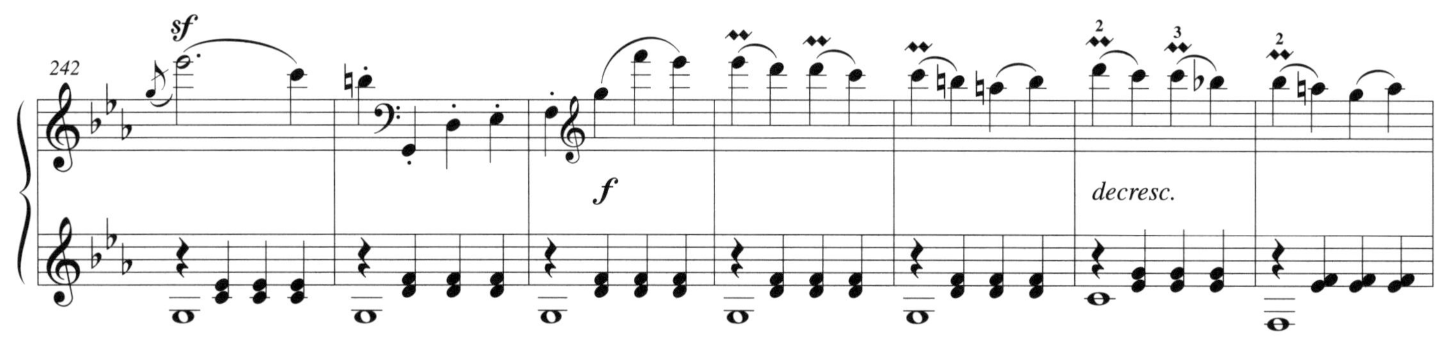
242
sf
f
decresc.

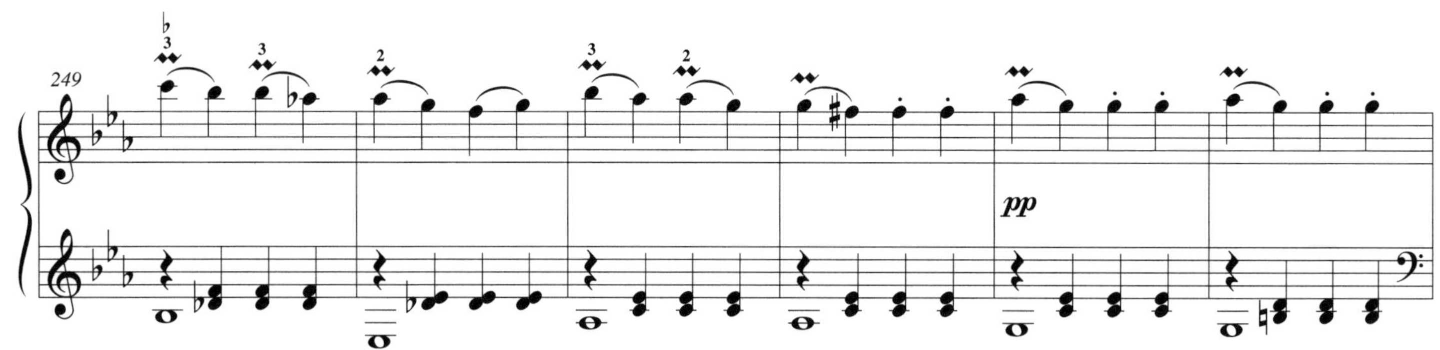
249
pp

255
p
259
cresc.
263
f
p
268
cresc.
272
276
f
p

281
cresc.
286
f
291
ff
297
Grave
p
cresc.
sf
decresc.
pp
301
Allegro molto e con brio
p
cresc.
306
ff

Second Movement

cresc.
p
pp
p
pp
cresc.
sf
sf

43
sf
fp
pp
46
49
sempre p
cresc.
p
52
55

59
62
65
68
71
pp
rfz
rfz
rfz
pp

SONATA IN D MAJOR

(No. 50, Hob. XVI/37, First Movement)

Franz Joseph Haydn
(1732-1809)

* may be played as a grace note:

Rondo alla Turca

from *Sonata in A Major, KV 331, Third Movement*

Wolfgang Amadeus Mozart
(1756-1791)

35
41
45
50
54
59
f

65
70
76
82
89
93
p
f
tr
1.
2.
Coda
f

97
(♪)
102
107
p
112
f
117
122

Sonata in B♭ major

(KV 570, First Movement)

Wolfgang Amadeus Mozart
(1756-1791)

Allegro

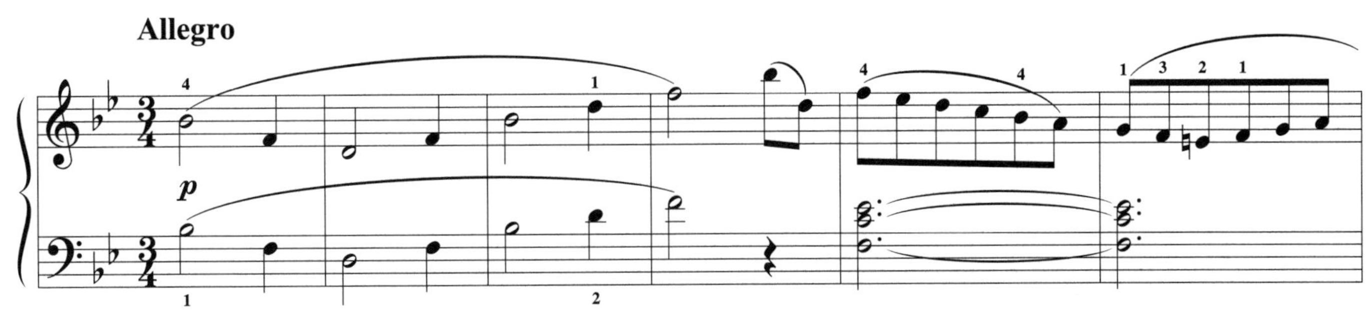

p
f
p

43
tr
48
52
56
tr
f
59

62
65
68
tr
p
72
76
f

f
p
f
p
tr
(♭)

145
150
156
161
166
170
176

tr
f
tr
p
f

Dreaming

(Opus 15, No. 3)

"Tu me parles du fond d'un rêve."

Amy Marcy Cheney Beach
(1867-1944)

N.B. The translation for Victor Hugo's quote is: "You speak to me from the depths of a dream."

decresc.
pp
poco rit.
a tempo
cresc. poco a poco
f
dim.
pp

8va
a tempo
rit.
mf
espressivo
cresc.
dim.
pp
pp molto delicato
dim.

cresc. poco a poco e appassionato
ff con rubato
sempre ff e dramatico

56

accel.

con rubato

59

8va

lunga

tranquillo

sff

stretto

rit.

mp

dolce

62

dim.

65

pp

sempre dim.

68

8va

rall.

ppp

Intermezzo

(Opus 118, No. 2)

Johannes Brahms
(1833-1897)

* Play the F sharp on the beat.

cresc.
cresc.
f
espressivo
p
dim.
calando
dolce
poco animato

41
45
Più lento
rit.
p
49
a tempo
53
rit.
Più lento
57
pp
una corda
ped. simile
rit.

61
rit.
65
Tempo I
cresc.
tre corde
ped. simile
69
f
73
p rit.
pp
77
rf
p

81
85
89
cresc.
93
cresc.
97
f
espressivo
p dim.

101
calando
dolce
cresc.
105
poco animato
109
113
rit.
Più lento
p

Dédiés à Madame Camille Pleyel

NOCTURNE

(Opus 9, No. 1)

Frédéric Chopin
(1810-1849)

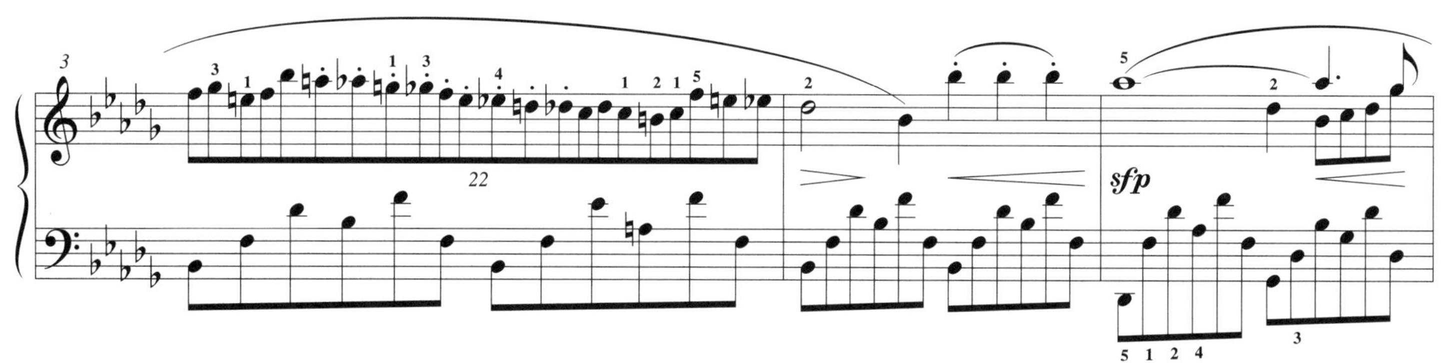

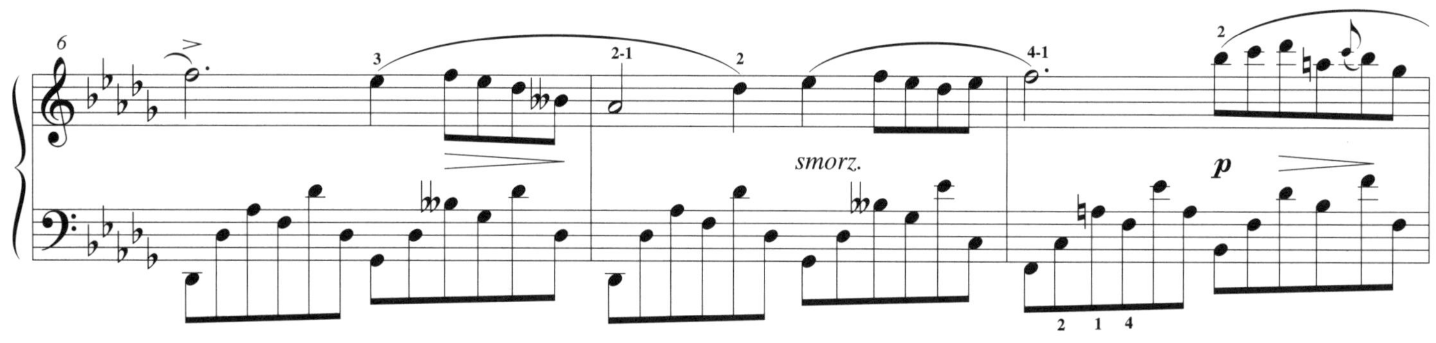

f appassionato
cresc.
con forza
p
sotto voce
smorz.
pp
simile
poco rall.
a tempo
ppp
f
cresc.

27
p
31
poco rall.
34
f
poco stretto
37
sfp
poco rall.
40
a tempo
f

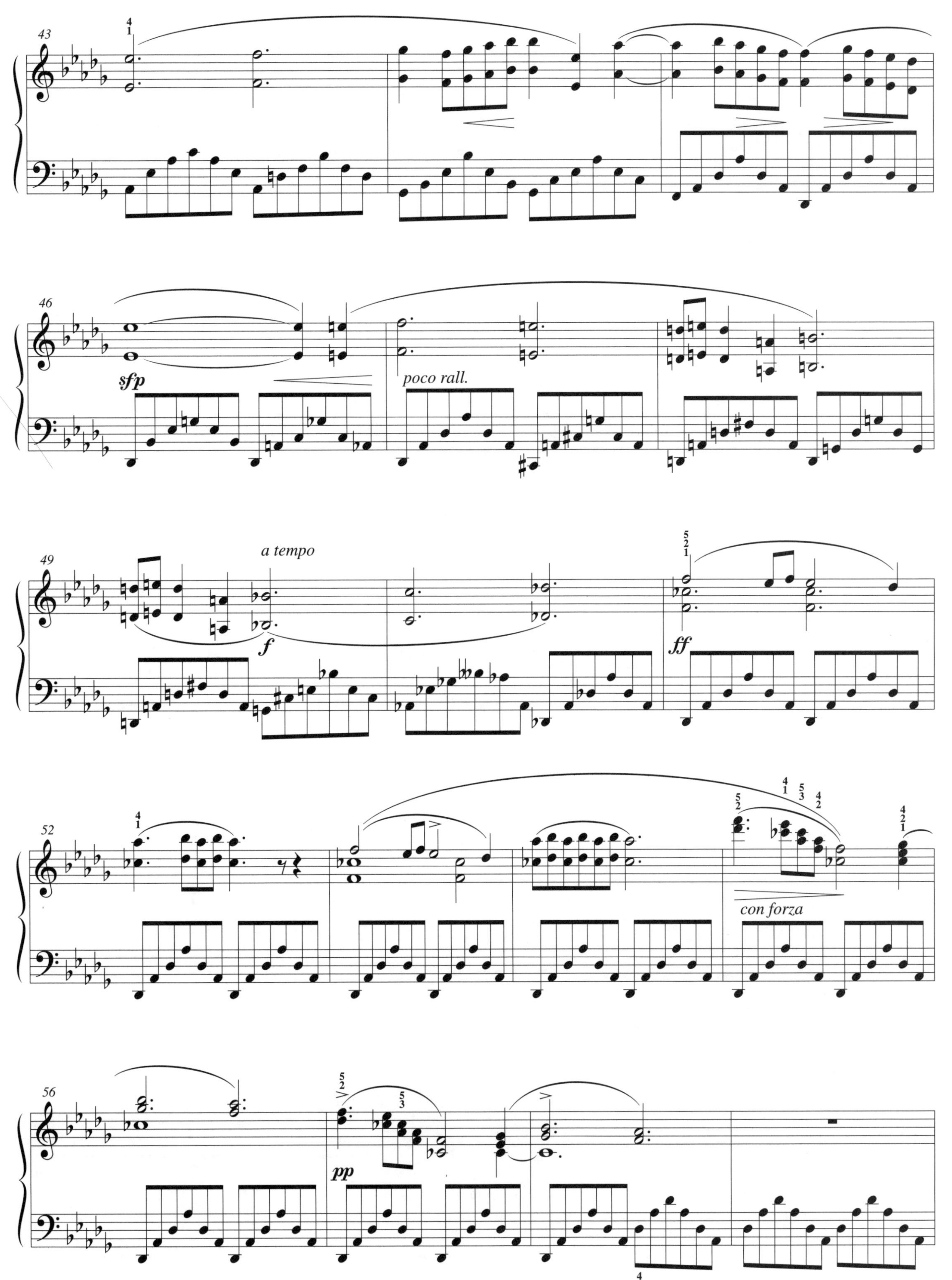

43
46
sfp
poco rall.
49
a tempo
f
ff
52
con forza
56
pp

ppp legatissimo
sempre pp
sf
smorz.
a tempo
rall. e dolciss.
8va

74
76
tr
f
78
cresc.
8va
ff
dim.
p
81
smorz.
ff
83
accel.
dim.
rit.
ppp

Consolation No. 5

Franz Liszt
(1811-1886)

espr. a piacere
cresc.

Mazurka

(Opus 59, No. 2)

Frédéric Chopin
(1810-1849)

dim.

54
59
fz
64
fz
fz
cresc.
69
p
f
74
ff
79
fz
f

83
cresc.
88
p
93
poco a
98
poco rall.
a tempo
102
106
pp

Wedding Day at Troldhaugen

from *Lyric Pieces for Piano, Opus 65, No. 6*

Edvard Grieg
(1843-1907)

17
20
f
23
dim.
pp dolce
26
f
29
dim.
pp
sempre pp

32
2
1

34
2
1
cresc.

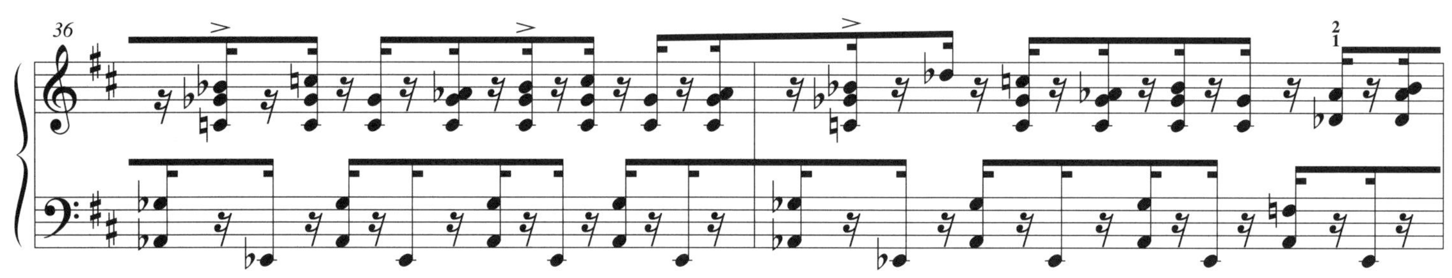
36
2
1

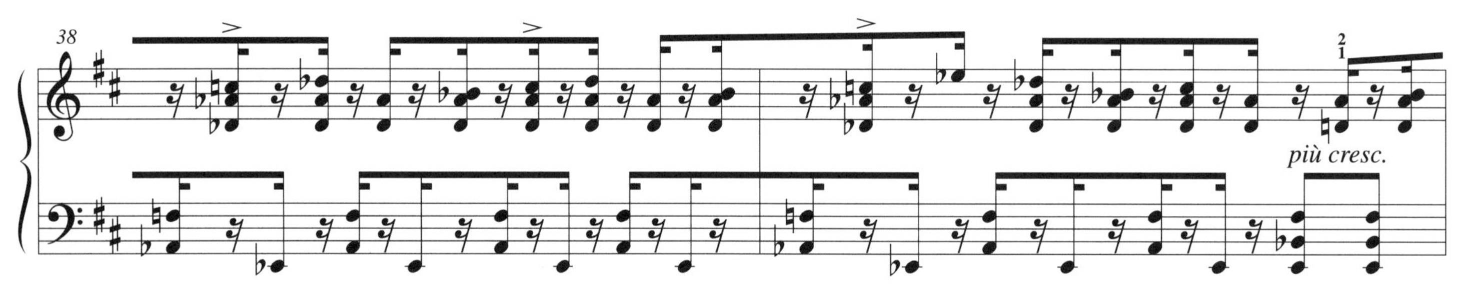
38
2
1
più cresc.

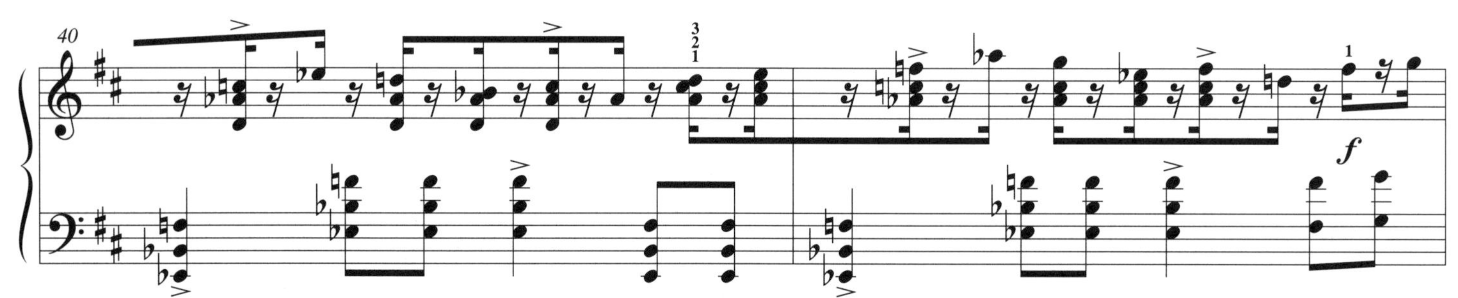
40
3
2
1
1
f

a tempo
marcato
più f
poco rit.
fff
fz
To Coda
ped. simile

Poco tranquillo
57
p
cantando
63
f
69
75
pp dolce
81

88
93
98
103
1.
2.
D.C. al Coda
Coda
fff sempre
staccato sempre
ped. simile

110
112
p
114
dim.
117
pp
121
dim.
ppp
fffz

Prelude in C♯ minor

(Opus 3, No. 2)

Sergei Rachmaninoff
(1873-1943)

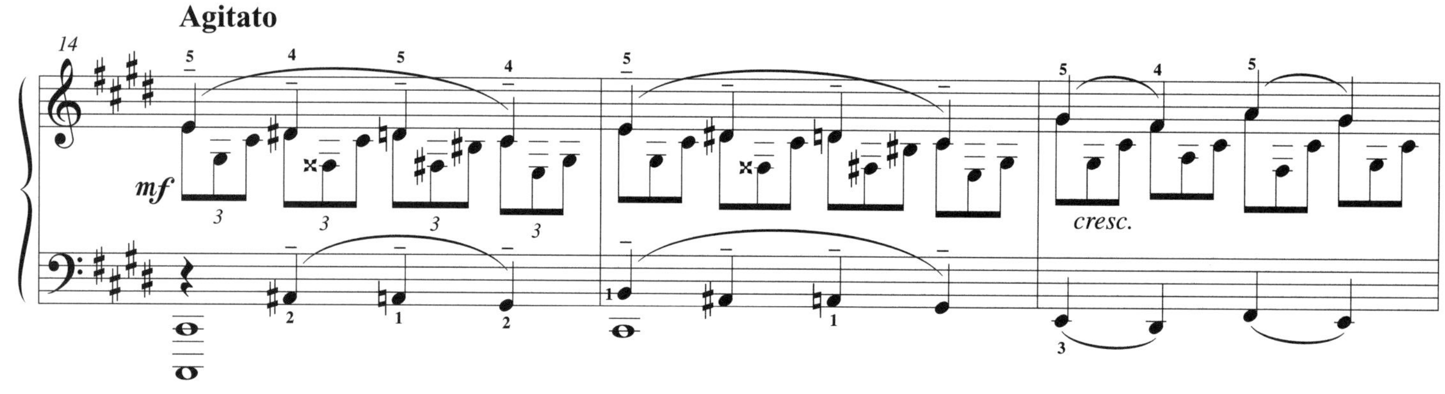
Agitato
14
mf
cresc.

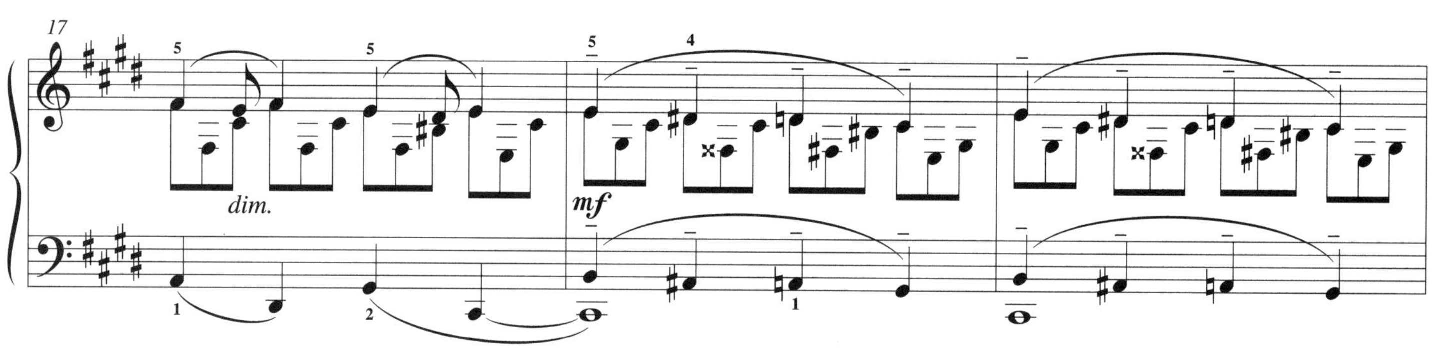
17
dim.
mf

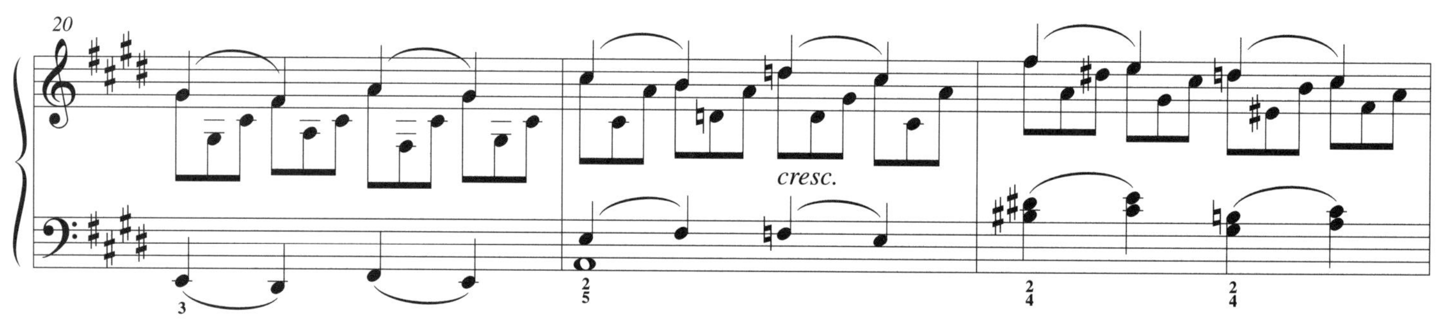
20
cresc.

23
dim.
cresc.

26
5
5
5
4
5
4
ff
29
4
2
5
5
dim.
32
5
4
cresc.
35
4
fff
3
3
2
4
1
3
2
4
1
3

38

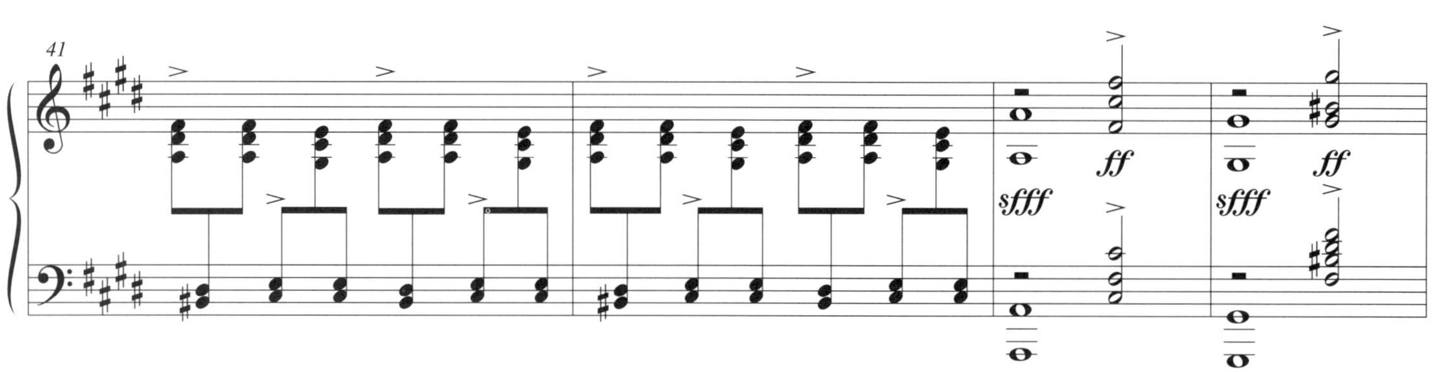
41
ff
sfff
ff
sfff

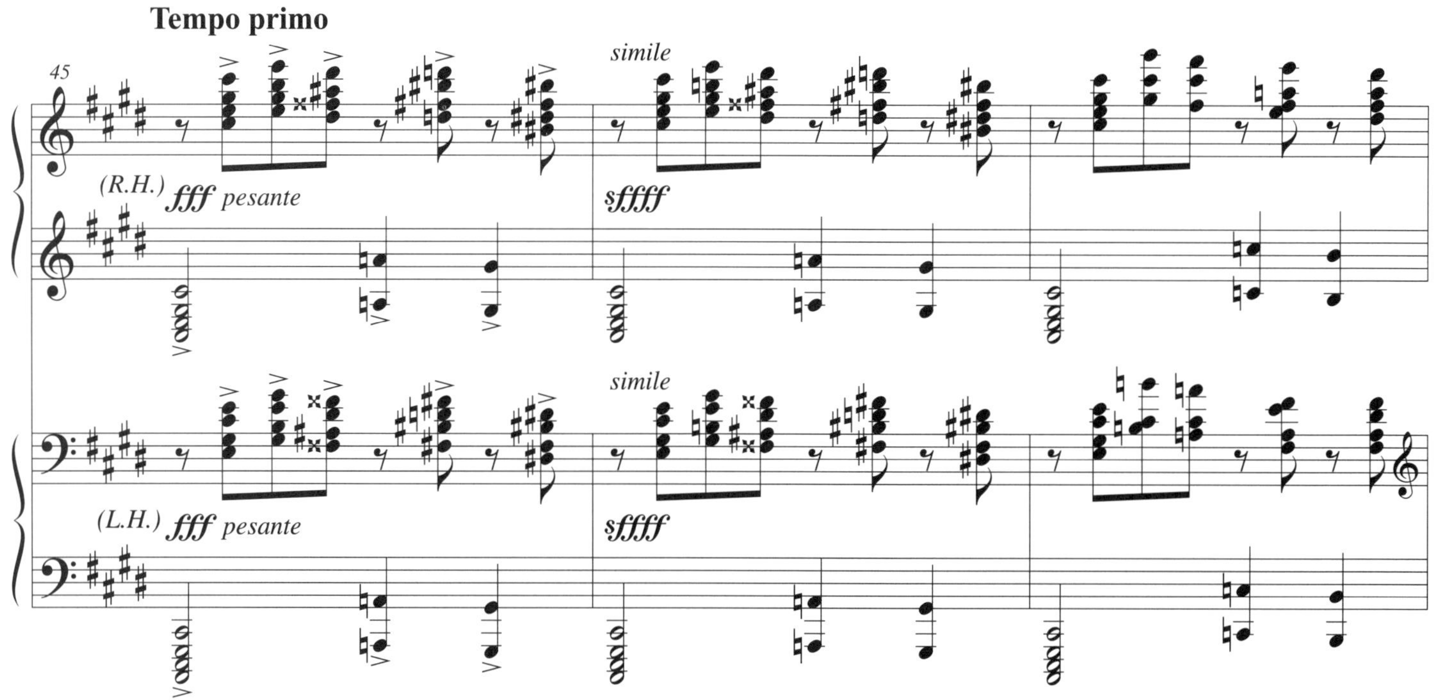
Tempo primo
45
simile
(R.H.) fff pesante
sffff
simile
(L.H.) fff pesante
sffff

* Play the lower C sharp octave as grace notes.

Poem No. 1

from *2 Poèmes, Opus 32*

Alexander Scriabin
(1872-1915)

Andante cantabile (♩. = 50)

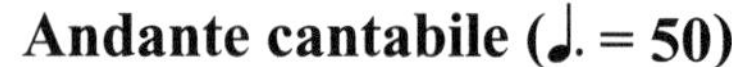

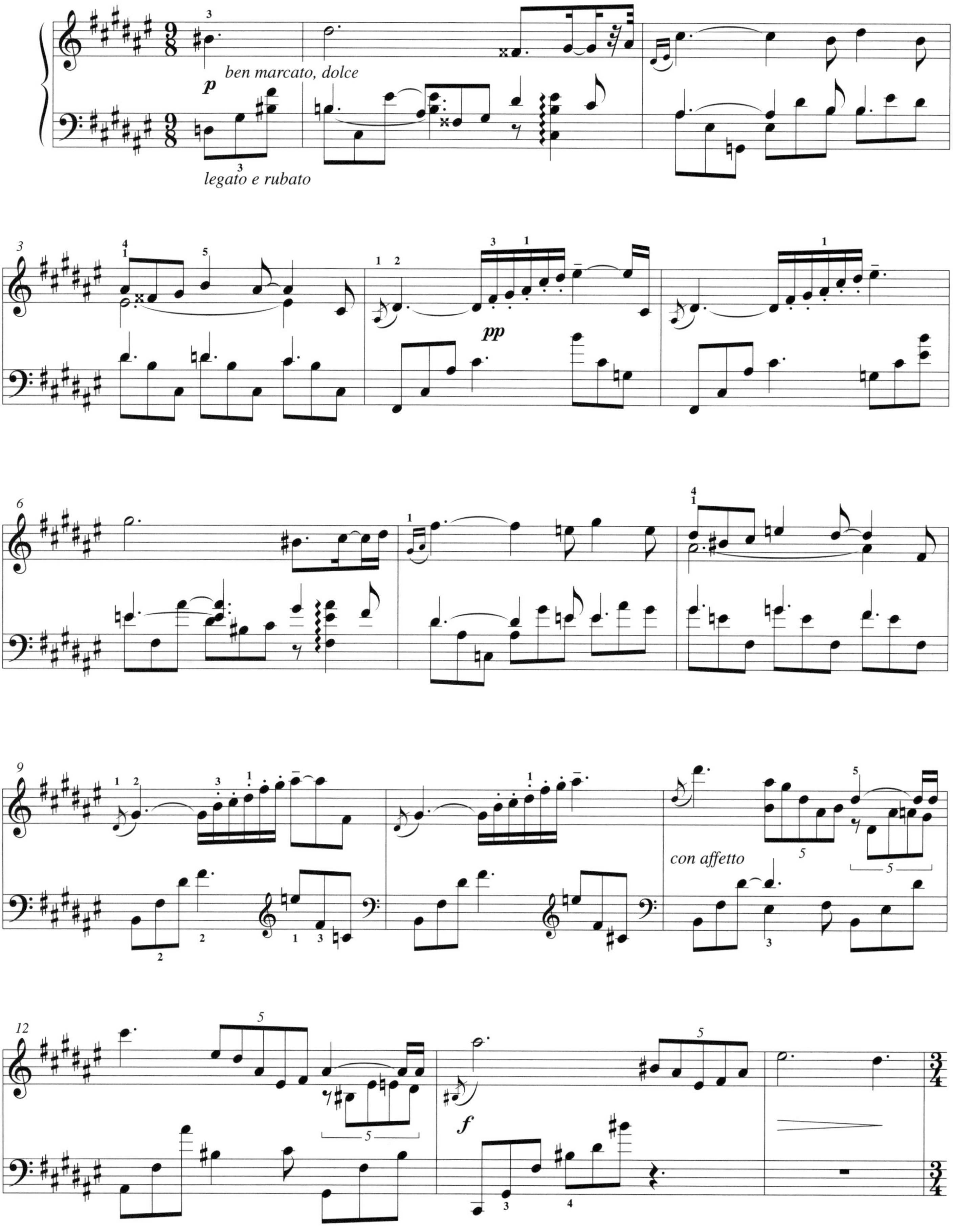

15
pp
17
cresc.
19
dim.
21
p
23
pp
p ben marcato, dolce

26
pp
29
32
con affetto
35
cresc.
5
5
37
rubato
f

39
pp
41
cresc.
43
dim.
45
pp
47
ppp

Capriccio

from *Pièces Brèves, Opus 84, No. 1*

Gabriel Fauré
(1845-1924)

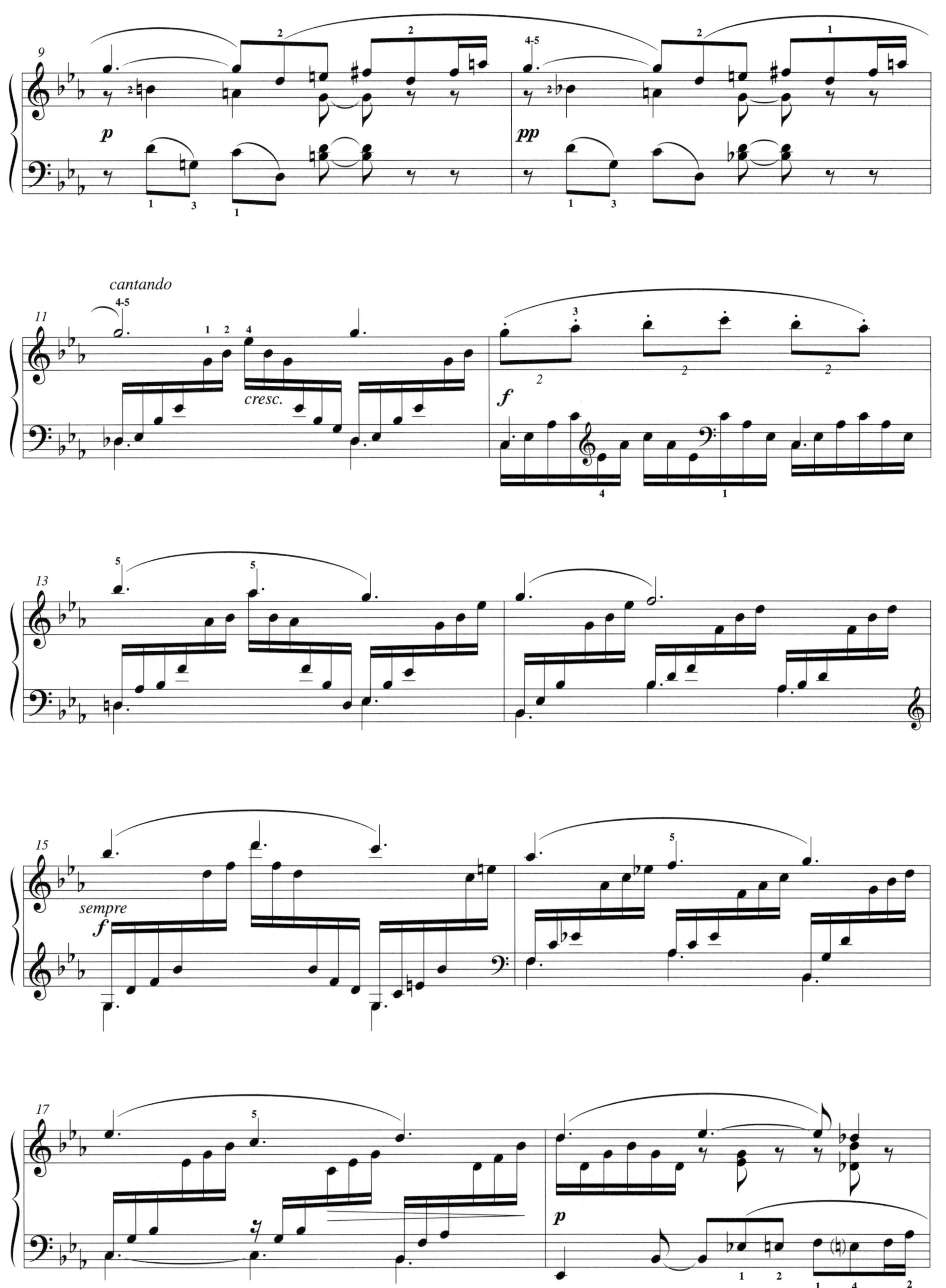

p
pp
cantando
cresc.
f
sempre
f
p

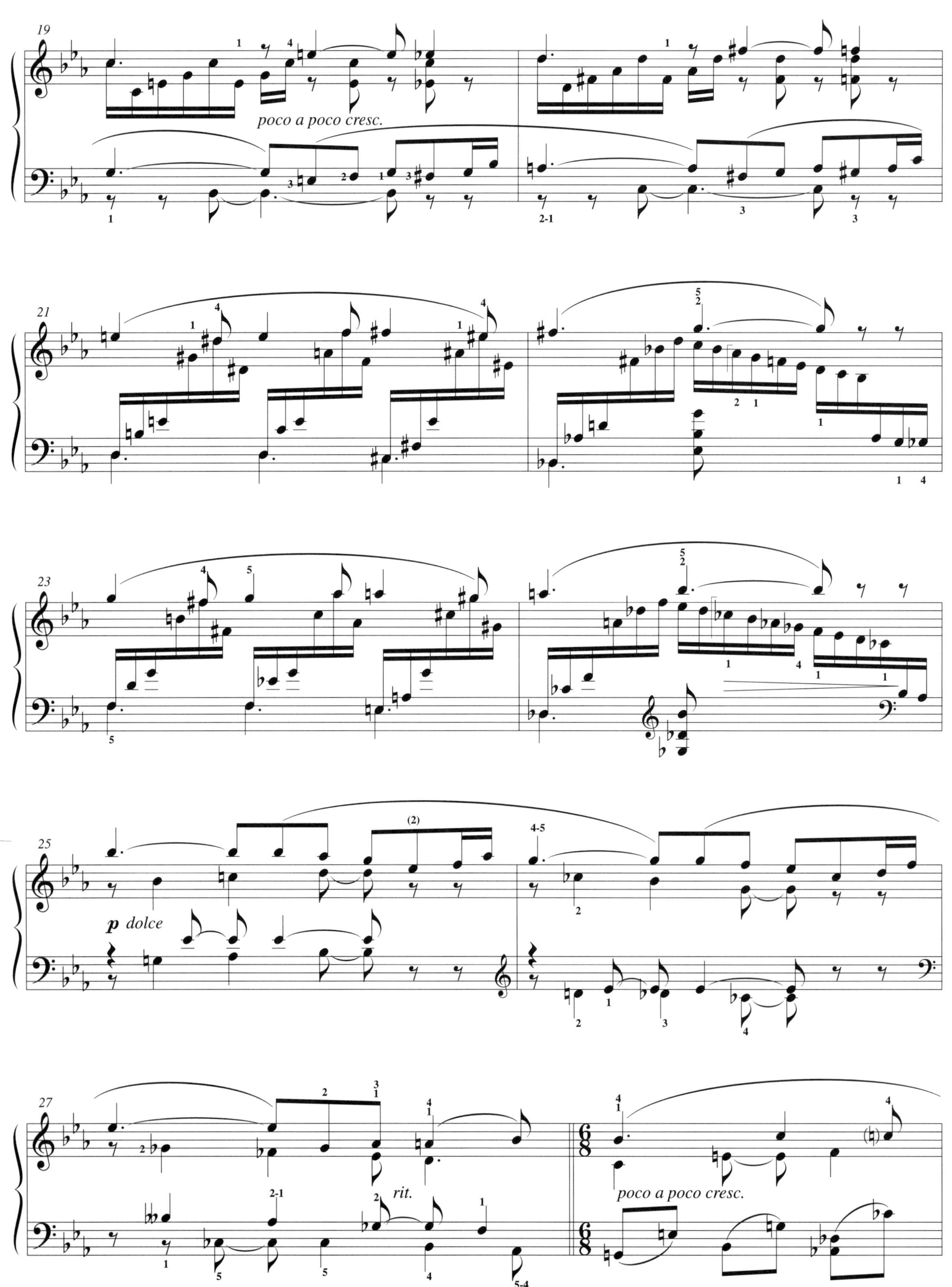
poco a poco cresc.
p dolce
rit.
poco a poco cresc.

29
32
f
33
34
dim.
35
36
p
37
38
dolce
39
poco rit.
a tempo

Romance
(Opus 24, No. 9)

Jean Sibelius
(1865-1957)

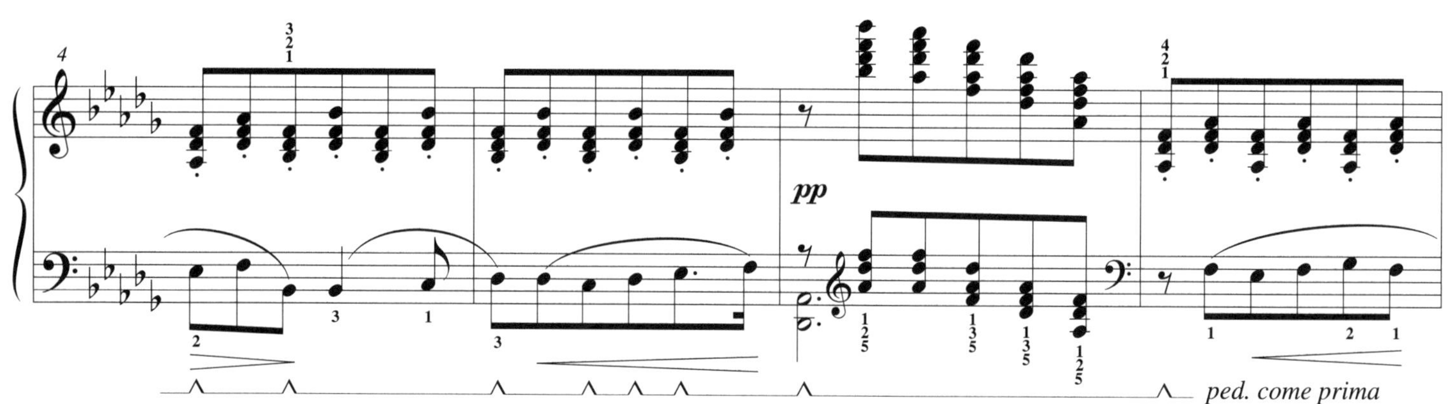

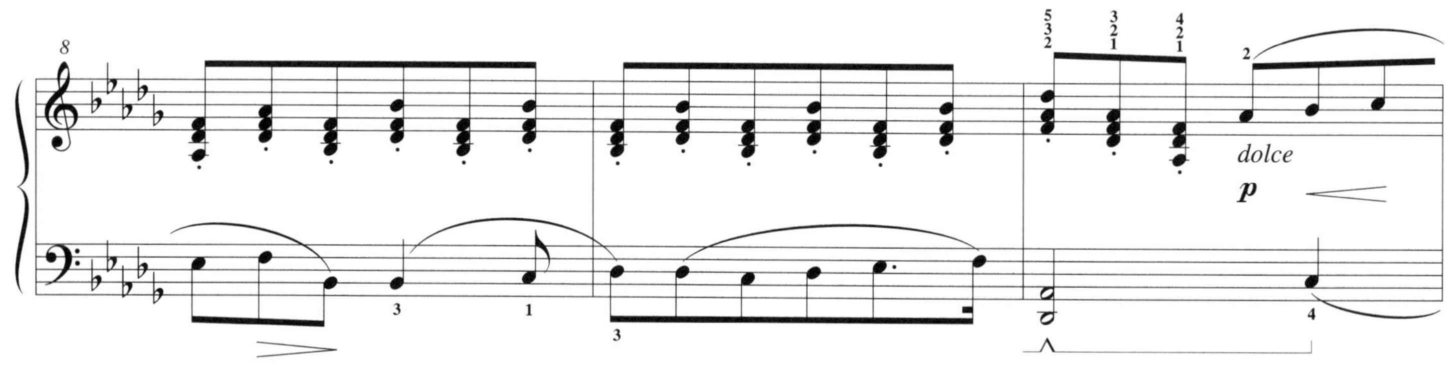

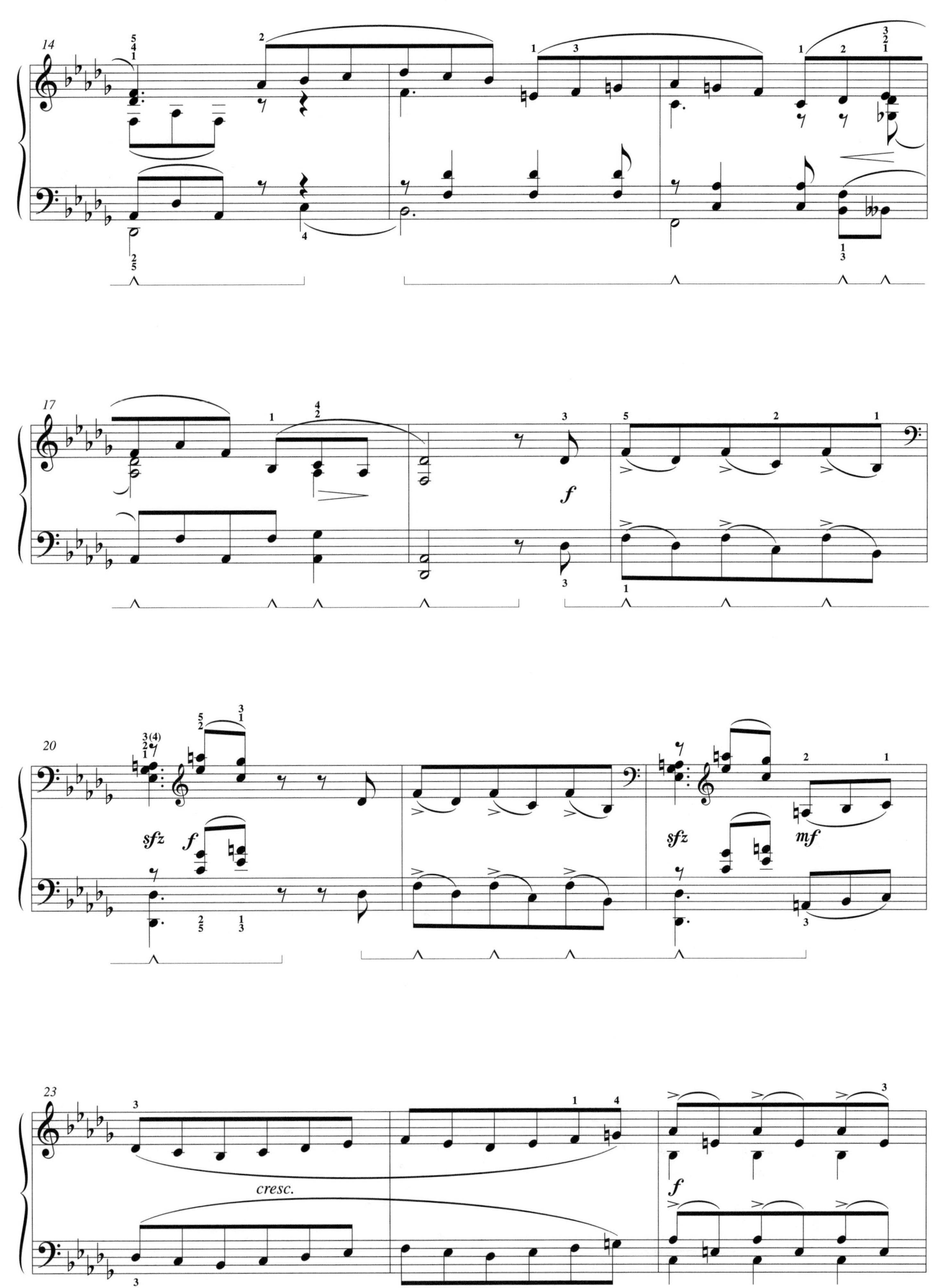
14
17
f
20
sfz
f
sfz
mf
23
cresc.
f

26
p
ped. simile

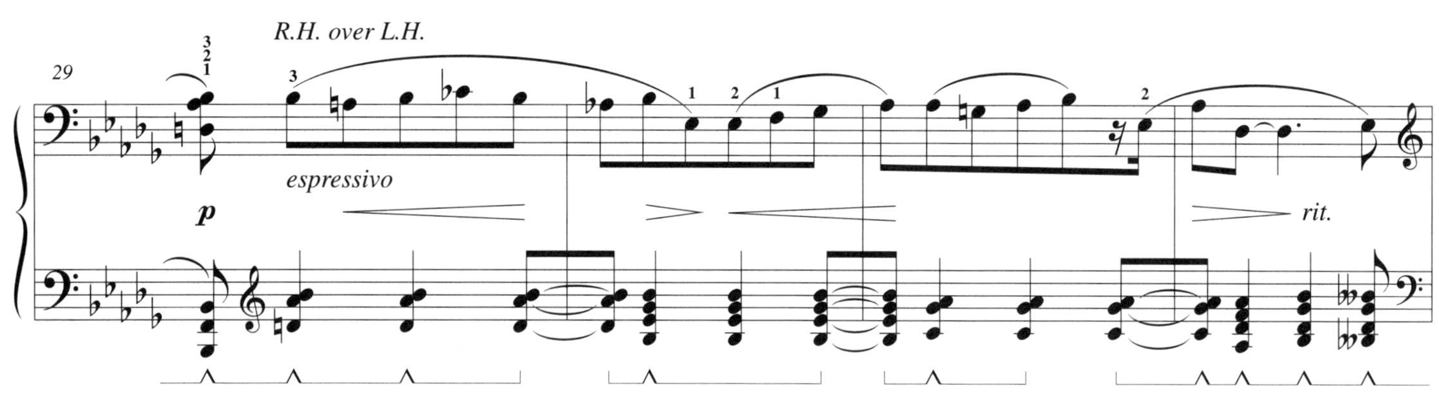
29
R.H. over L.H.
espressivo
p
rit.

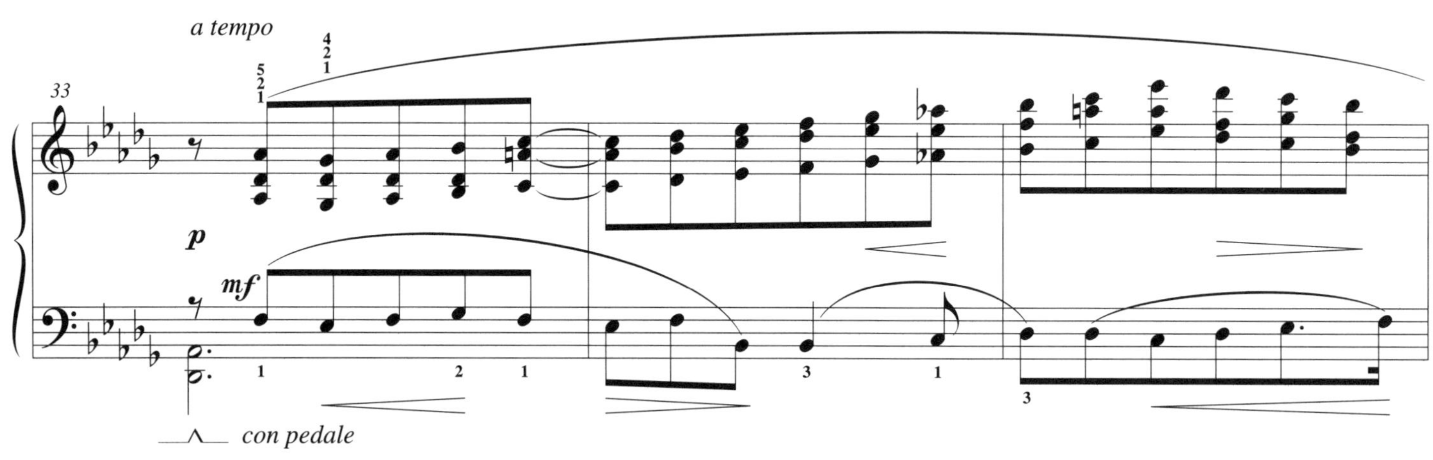
a tempo
33
p
mf
con pedale

36
p
mf

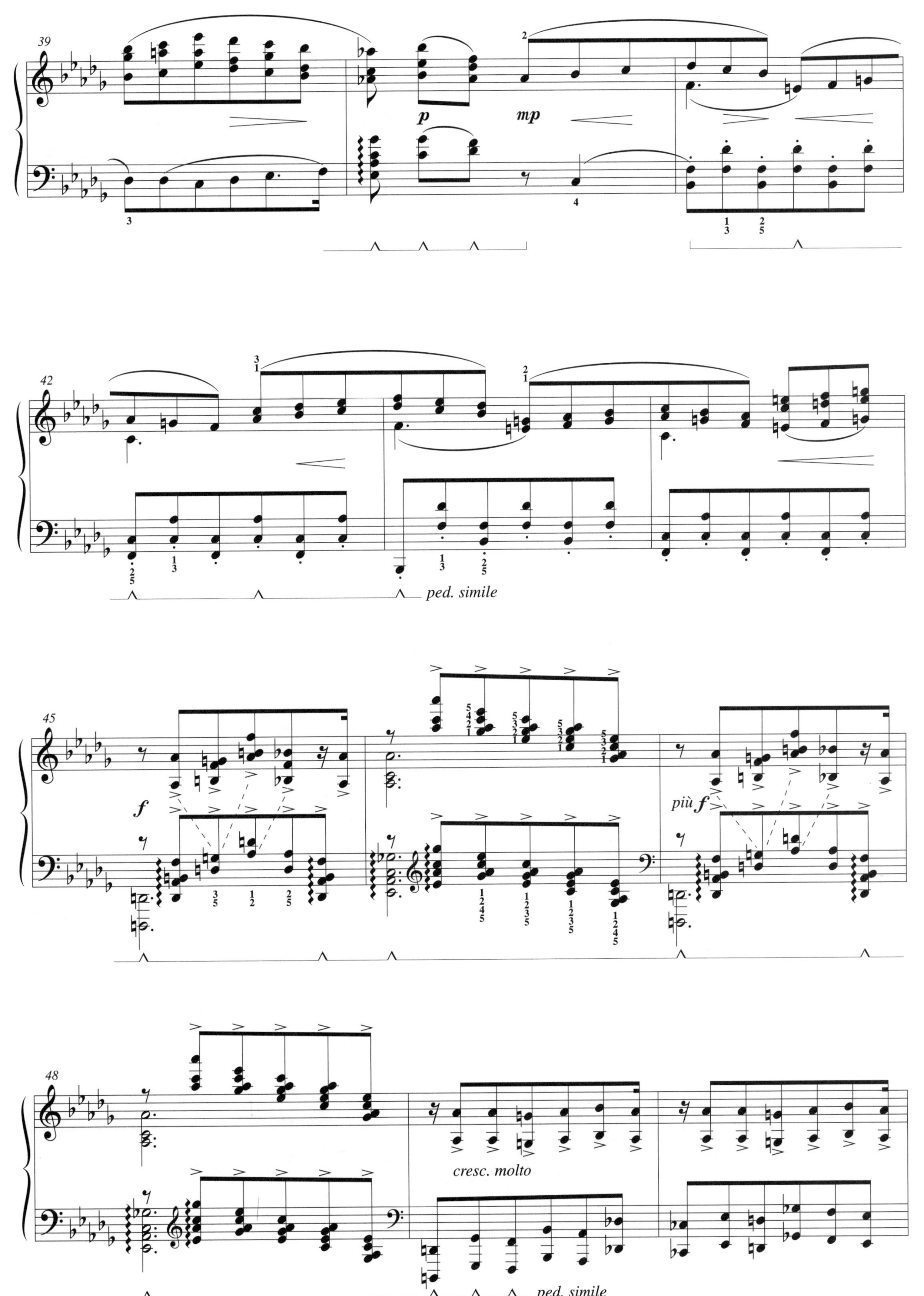
39
p
mp
42
ped. simile
45
f
più f
48
cresc. molto
ped. simile

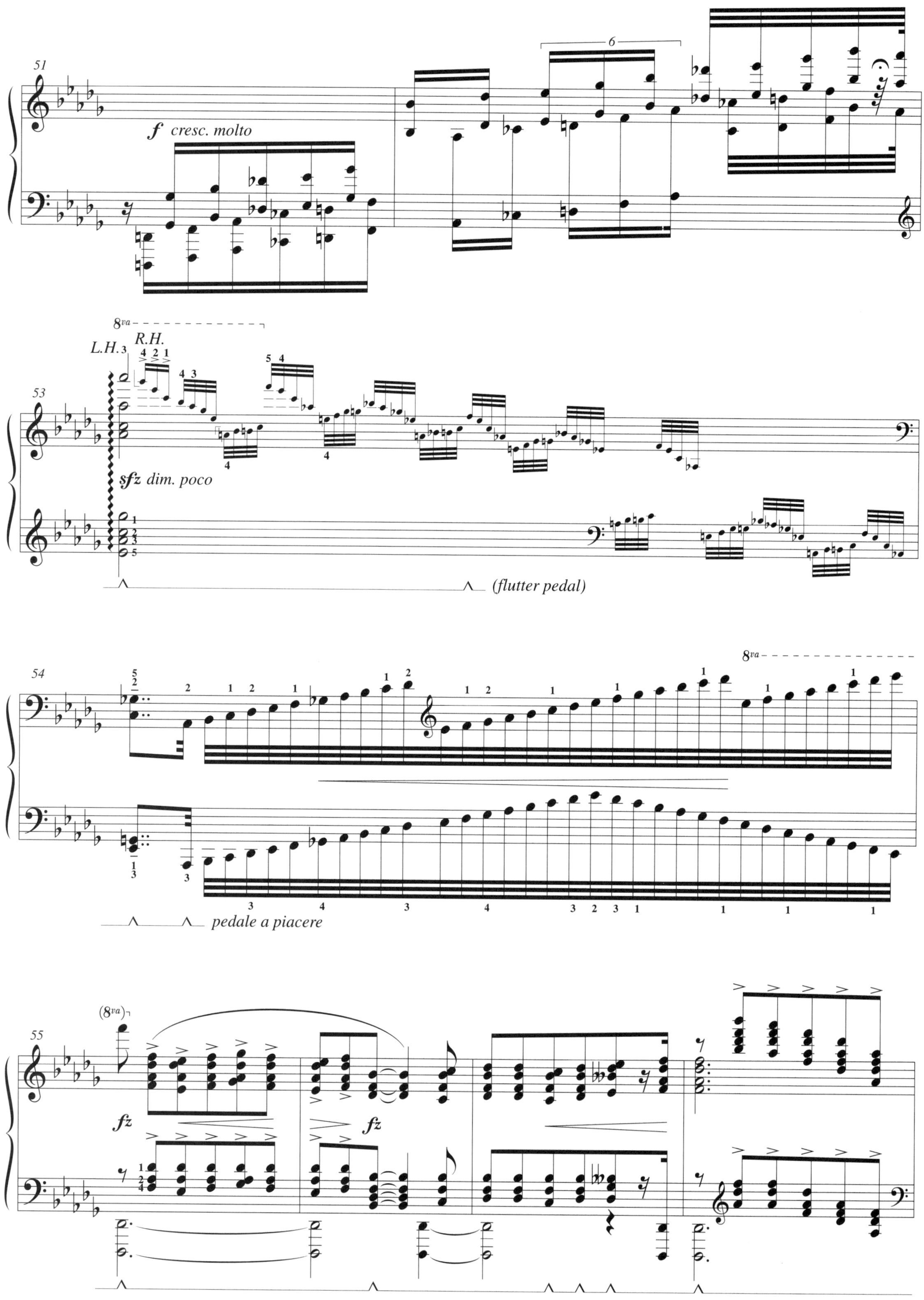
51
f cresc. molto
6
53
8va
L.H. 3
R.H.
sfz dim. poco
(flutter pedal)
54
8va
pedale a piacere
55
(8va)
fz
fz

meno f
mp
più p
mf
mf
mp poco rit.

Etude de Sonorite No. 1

François Morel
(1926-)

8
p
rubato
8va
11
8va
R.H.
L.H.
over
8va
3
13
dolce sensible (sensitively)
dolce subito
p
L.H.
ped. simile

16
18
délicat
(delicately)
L.H.
(p)
f secco (without pedal)
21
sonore (ringing)
mp
lointain
(distant)
serrez (tightly)
R.H.
L.H.
24
R.H.
L.H.
f
mf
dim.

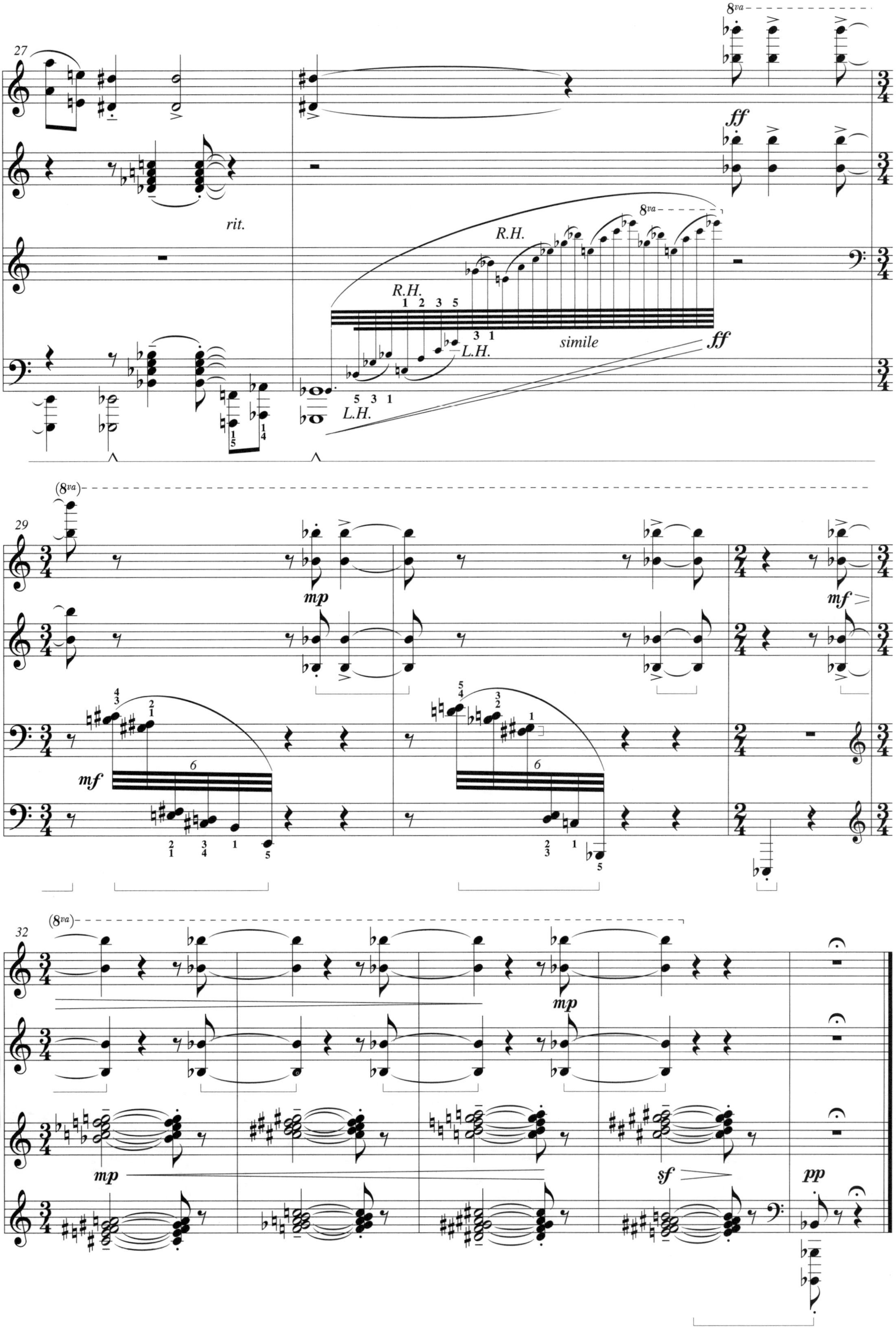

27

8va

ff

rit.

R.H.

8va

R.H.

1 2 3 5

3 1

simile

L.H.

ff

5 3 1

L.H.

1 5

1 4

(8va)

29

mp

mf

4 3

2 1

mf

6

2 1

3 4

1

5

5 4

3 2

1

6

2 3

1

5

(8va)

32

mp

mp

sf

pp

Clair de lune

Moonlight, from *Suite bergamasque*

Claude Debussy
(1862-1918)

Tempo rubato
R.H.
peu à peu cresc. et animé (louder and livelier)
8va
dim. molto
Un poco mosso

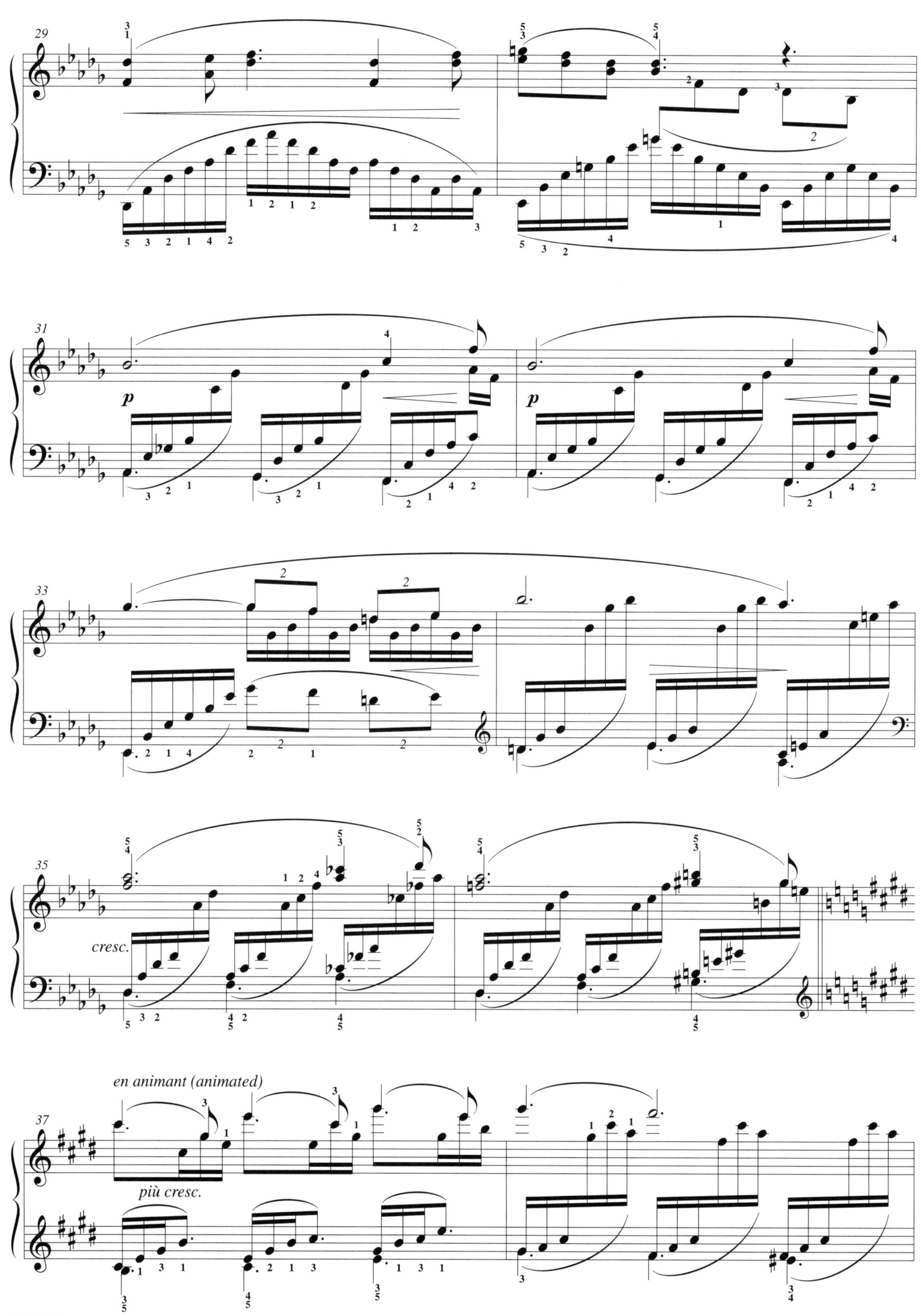
p
p
cresc.
en animant (animated)
più cresc.

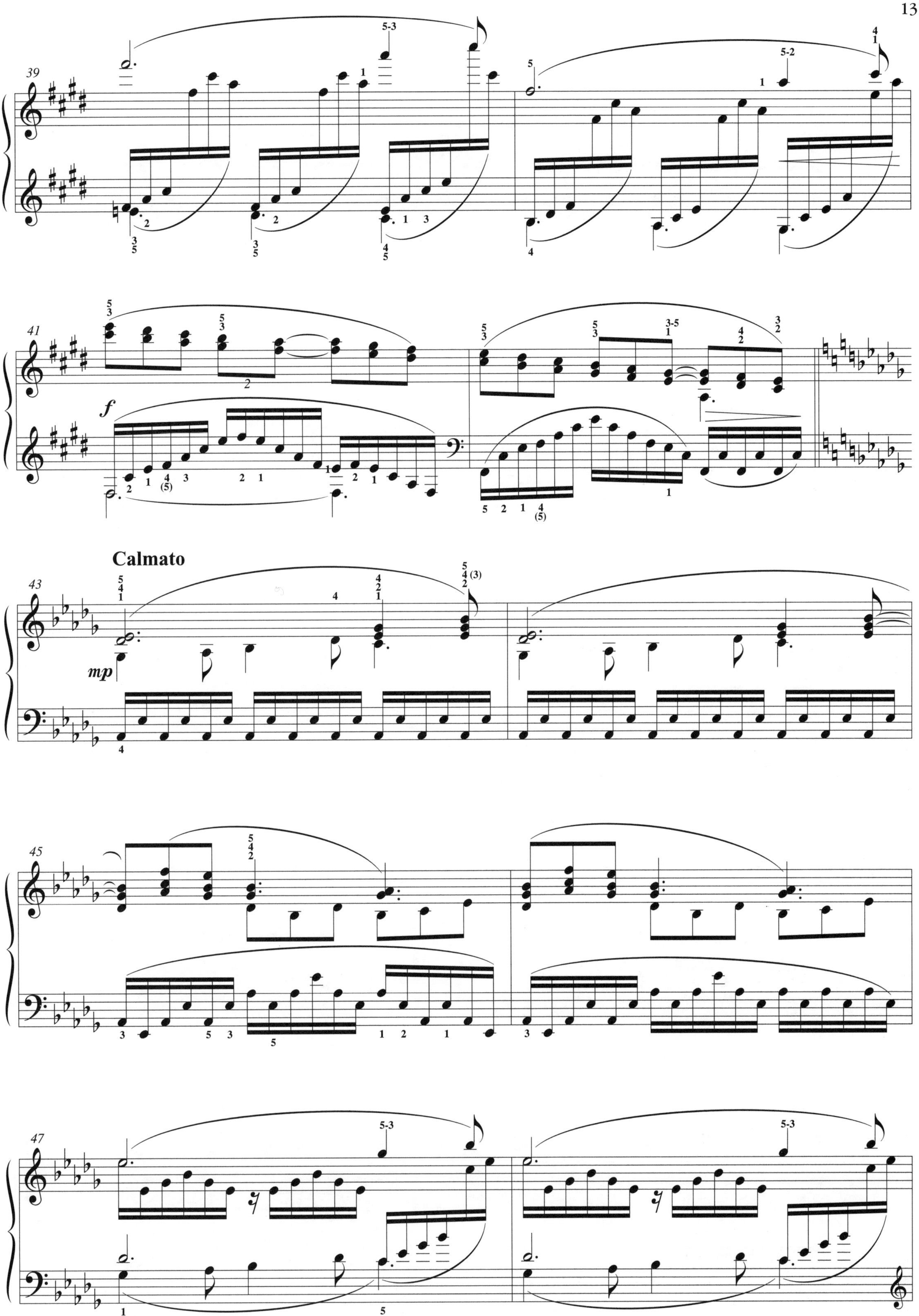

39

41

f

Calmato

43

mp

45

47

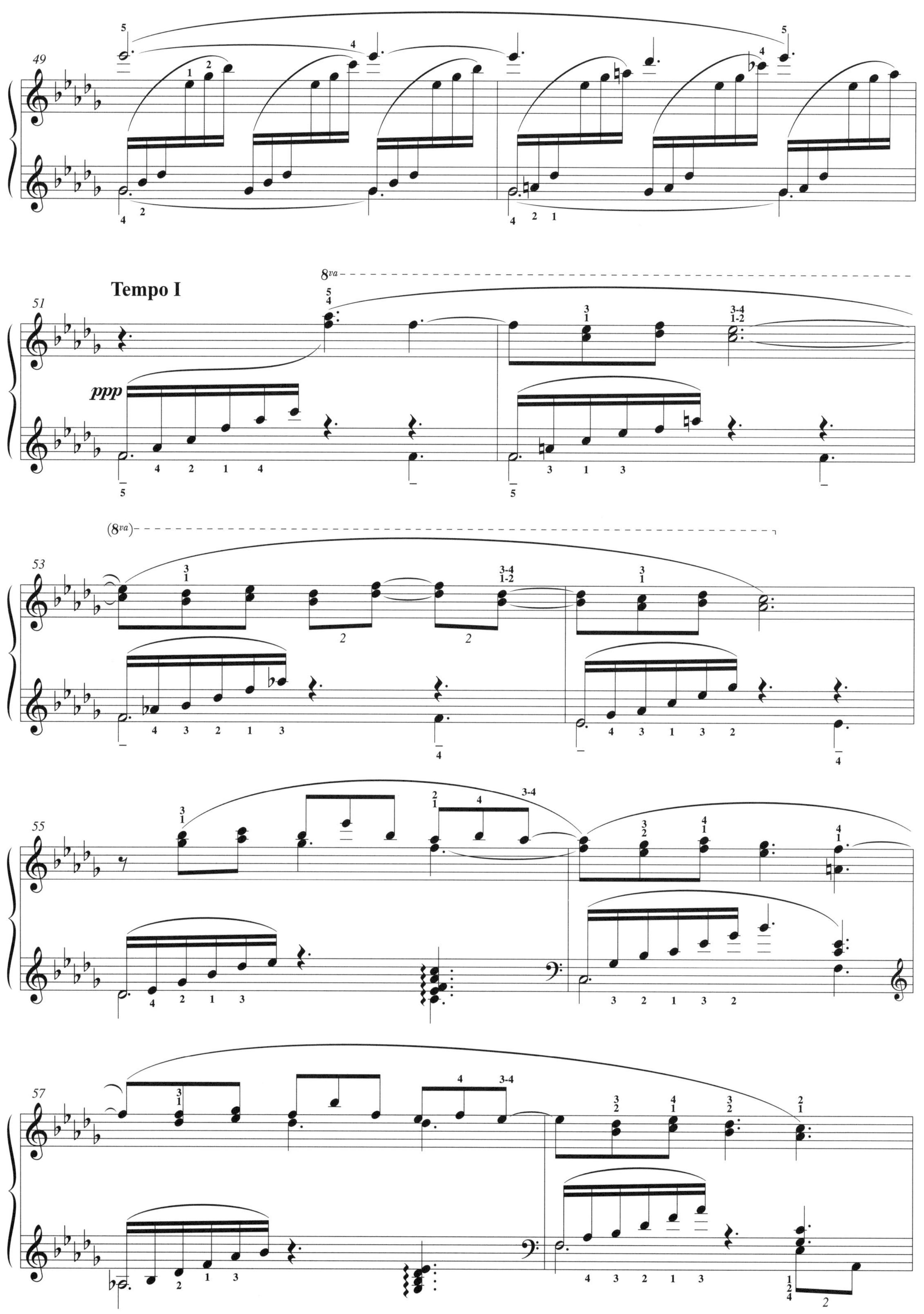
Tempo I
ppp
8va
(8va)

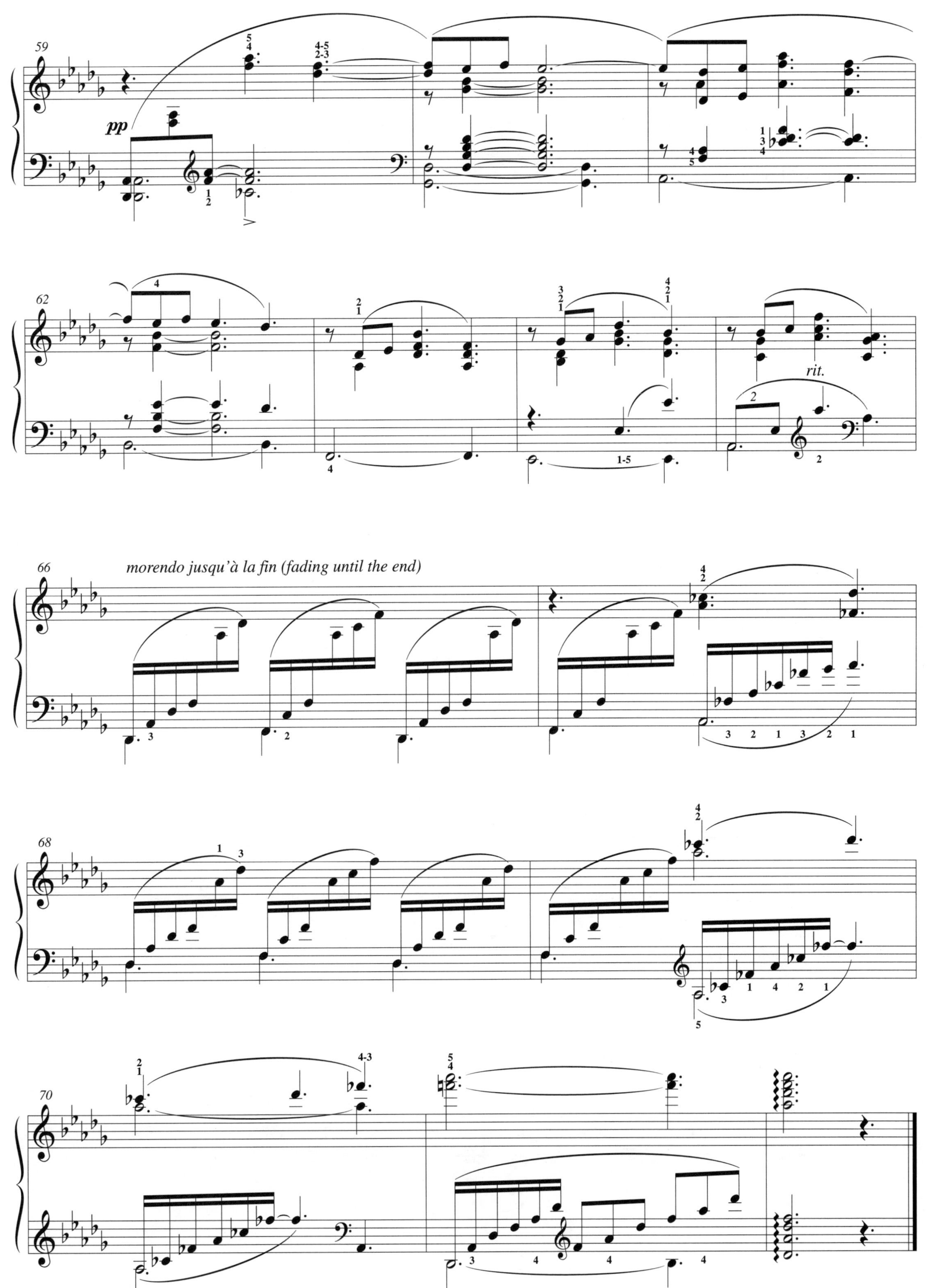

pp
rit.
morendo jusqu'à la fin (fading until the end)

The Cat and the Mouse

(Scherzo Humoristique)

Aaron Copland
(1900-1990)

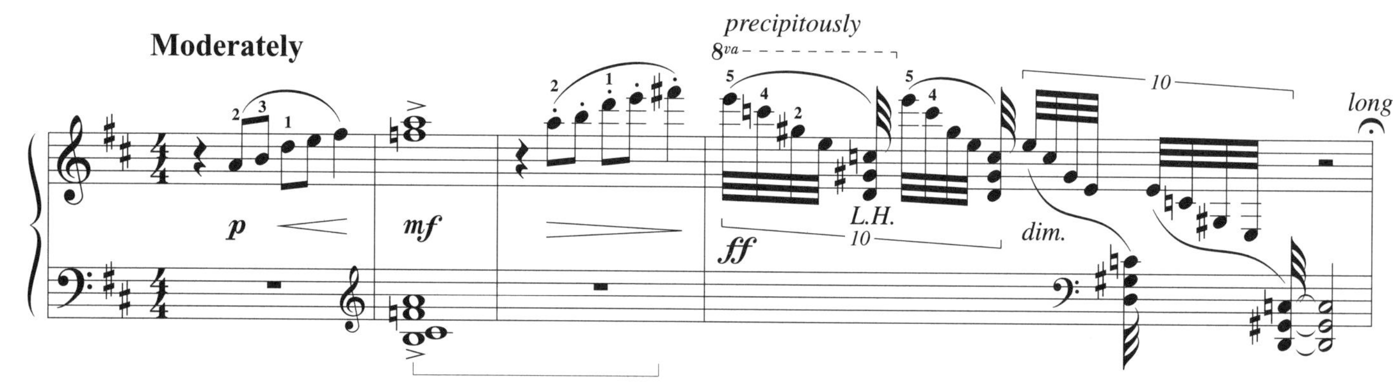

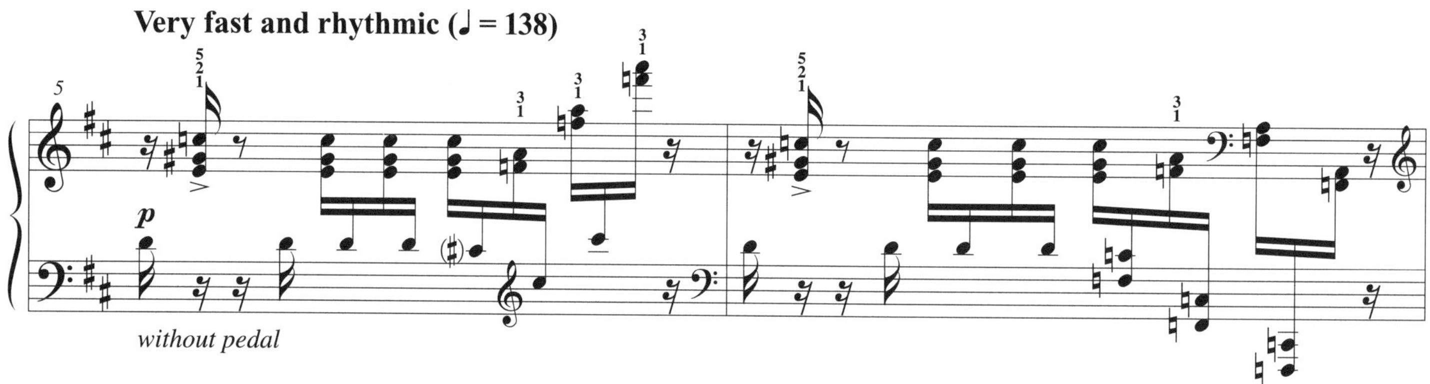

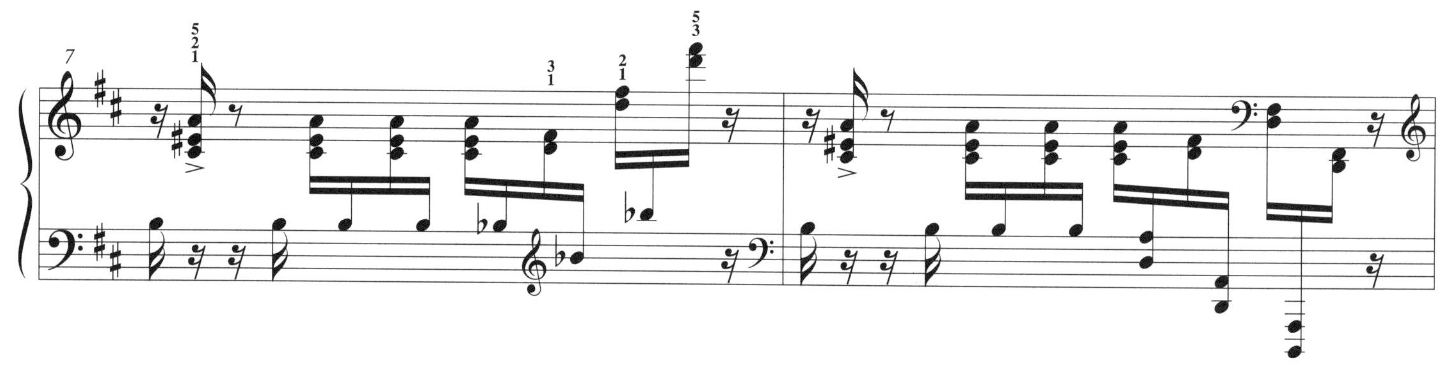

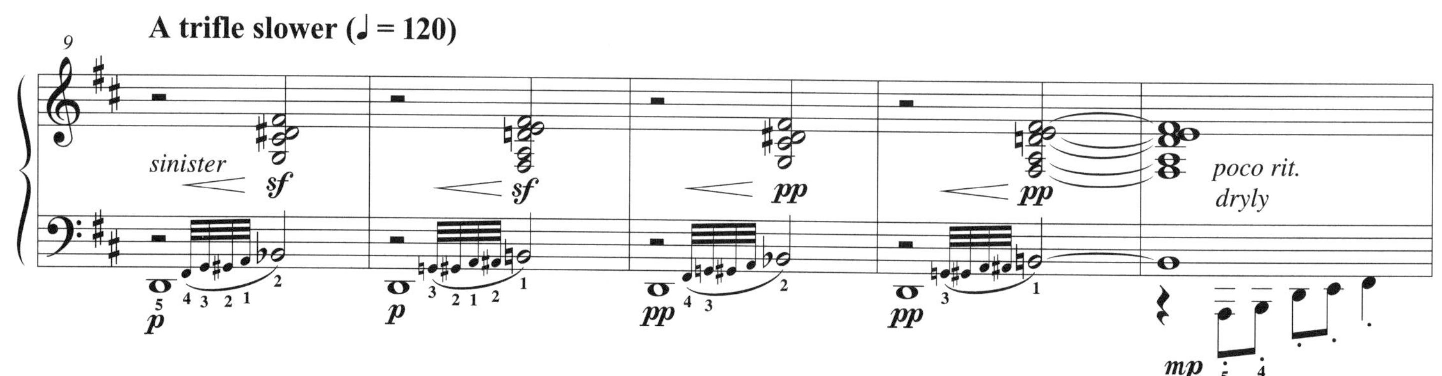

a tempo (♩ = 138)
8va
gliss.
f
ff
long
Still faster (♩ = 160)
R.H.
mf
(L.H. above)
p
8va
R.H.
L.H.
p

short

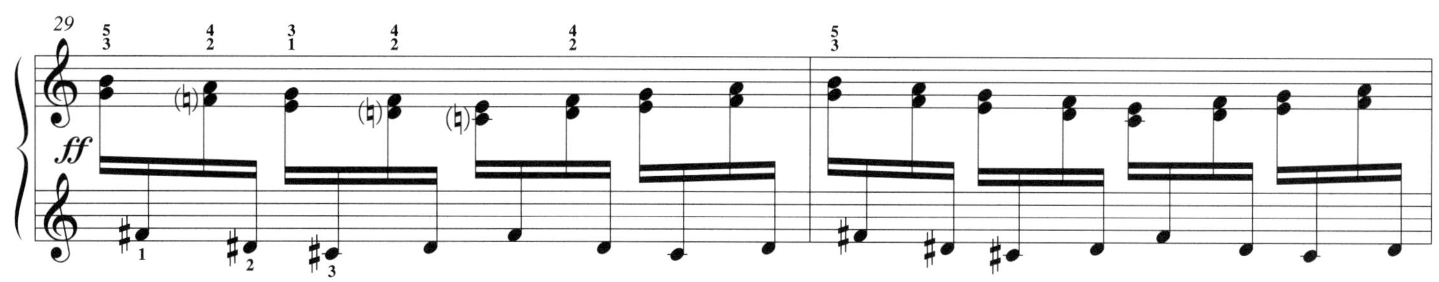
ff

Very much slower (♩ = 88)
p
ppp
p
f

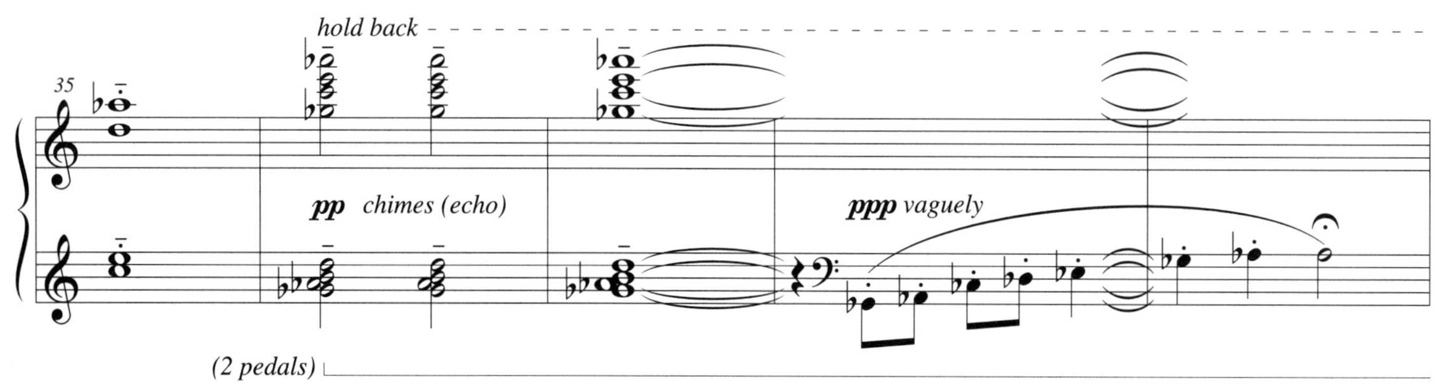
hold back
pp chimes (echo)
ppp vaguely
(2 pedals)

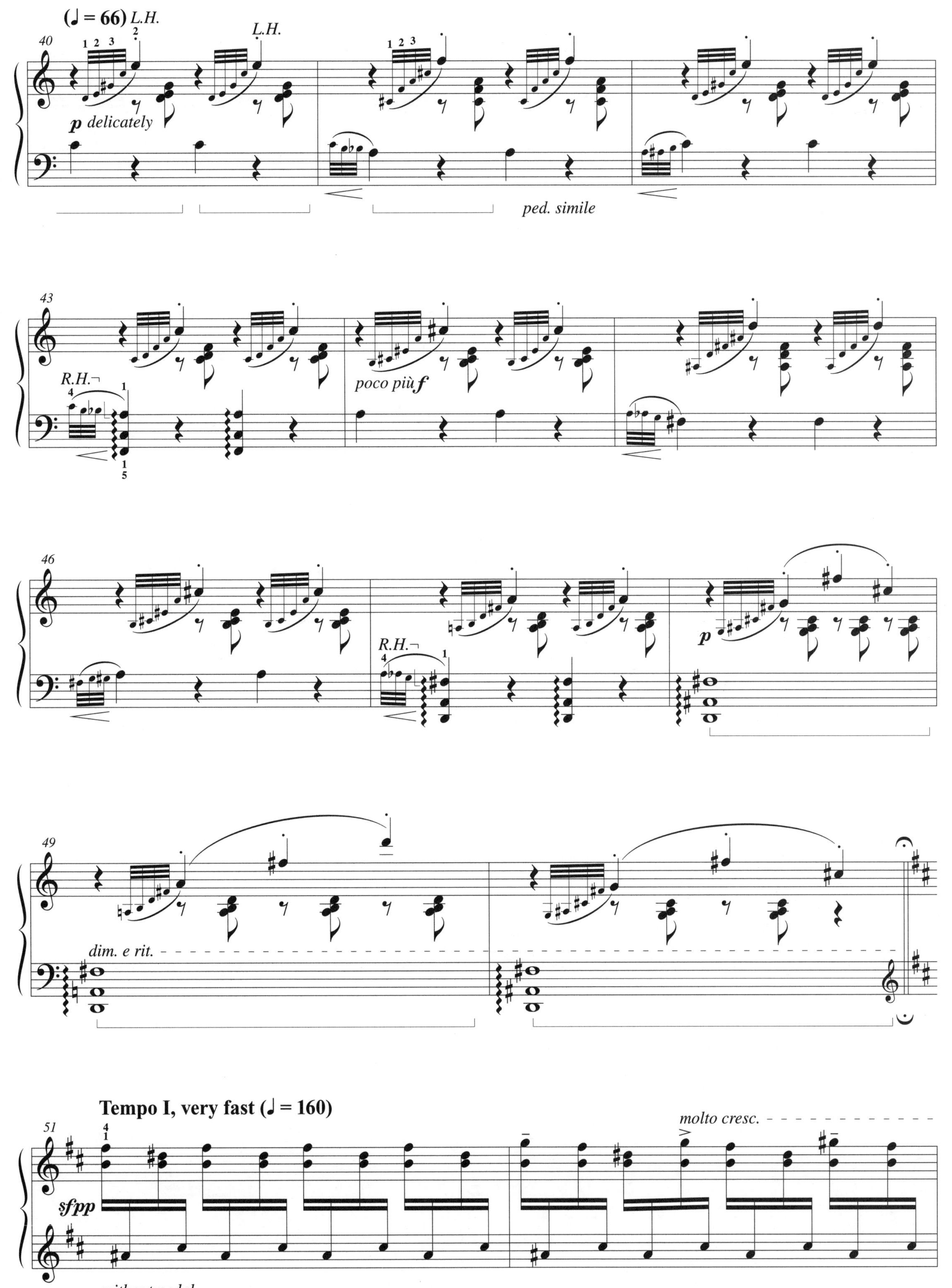
(♩ = 66) L.H.
L.H.
p delicately
ped. simile
R.H.
poco più f
R.H.
p
dim. e rit.
Tempo I, very fast (♩ = 160)
molto cresc.
sfpp
without pedal

53
(♩ = 138)
55
ff
8va
57
59
mf
sf
f
62
R.H.
gliss.
Dry, heavy

*Depress sostenuto pedal.

Rialto Ripples

(Rag)

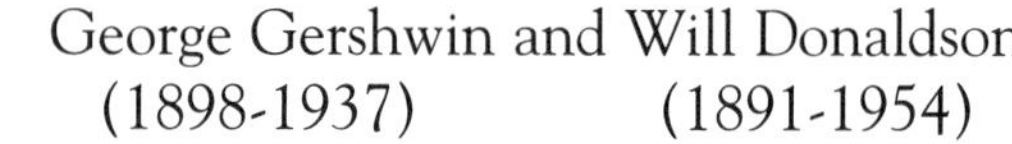

Marcato

mf

f

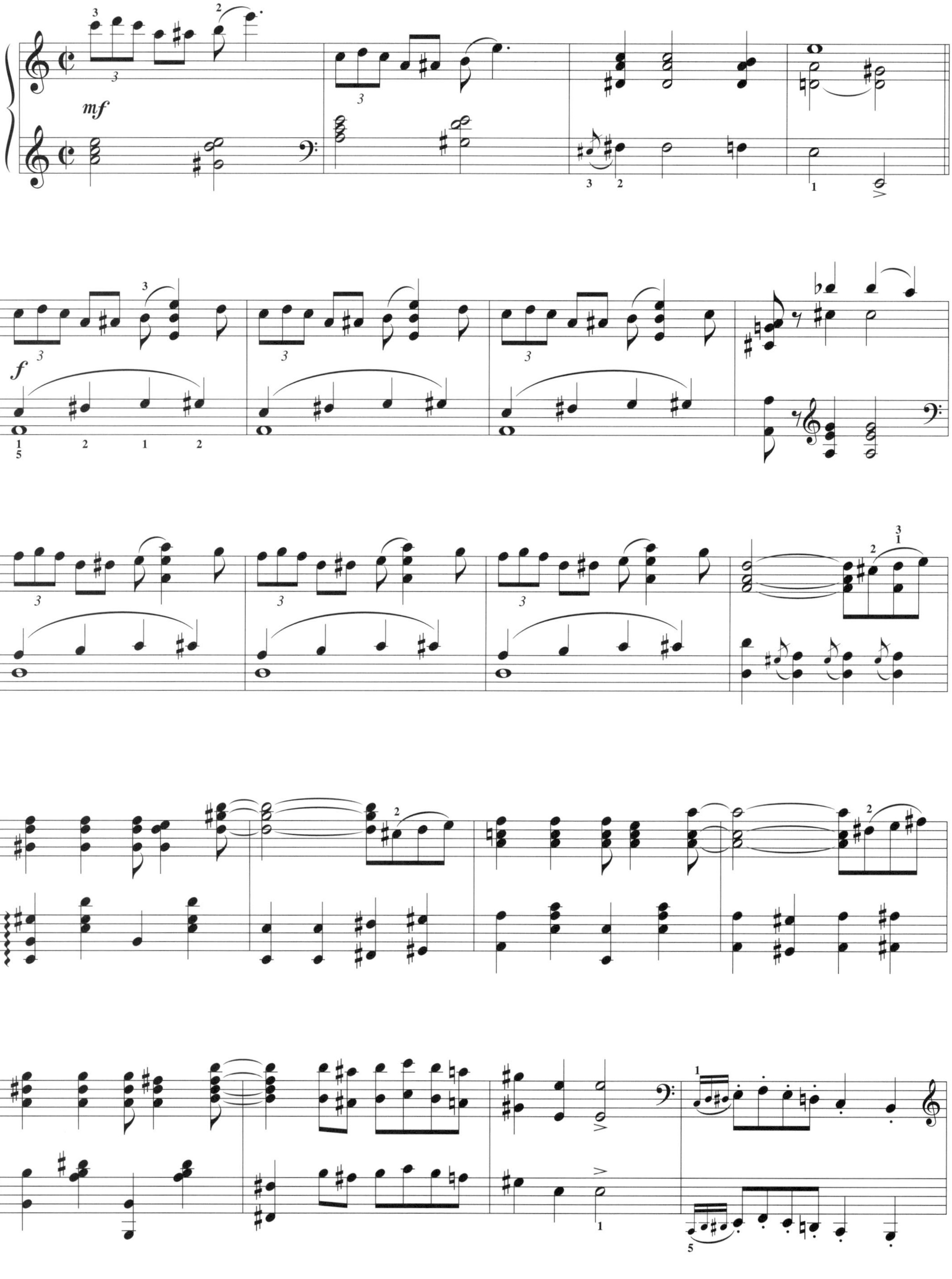

mf

ff
Fine
8va

Trio
mf
ff
fz
mf
ff
mf
D.S. al Fine

Minuet on the Name of Haydn

(Menuet sue le nom de Haydn)

Maurice Ravel
(1875-1937)

N.B. Can you find “HAYDN” in measures 27-28? And anywhere else?

Bulgarian Dance No. 2

from *Six Dances in Bulgarian Rhythm*

Béla Bartók
(1881-1945)

* *N.B.* Use quarter pedal.

21
cresc.
f martell.
25
sf
marc.
29
mf
dim.
sff
33
mp
37
p

rit.
a tempo
più p
mf
mp
ppp
pp

About the Pieces and the Composers

BAROQUE ERA

Allemande (from *French Suite No. 5, BWV 816*), by Johann Sebastian Bach (1685-1750)
An *allemande* is a stately German dance, from *Allemagne,* the French name for the country of Germany. Bach composed six *French Suites* while he was employed in the court at Cöthen under Prince Leopold. As a young boy, Leopold asked his parents to bring music into the royal home. Through his own love of music and his musical education, Leopold was highly appreciative of Bach, who composed many concertos, sonatas and suites for the prince's entertainment. The French Suites appear among the keyboard compositions in the *Clavierbüchlein für Anna Magdalena Bach,* a notebook of piano pieces which Bach gave to his wife around 1722, and which he had completed by 1725. Bach also completed the famous *Brandenburg Concertos* while at Cöthen.

Courante (from *French Suite No. 5, BWV 816*), by Johann Sebastian Bach (1685-1750)
In French, *courante* means "running." In music the *courante* is a flowing, fast-paced dance in triple meter. The Baroque era was a period of innovation. Dance music was transformed into elegant entertainment. The baroque orchestral suite consisted of dance themes ranging from the stately to the lively to the graceful, written in the same key. Bach's harpsichord suites are among the best examples of the baroque suite. Bach spent much of his professional life in the service of the church. He believed that all his work was done in the service of God, so he did not make a distinction between sacred and secular activity. His familiar *Air on a G String* is from an orchestral suite that premiered at a coffee house.

Sonata *(K.87, L.33),* by Domenico Scarlatti (1685-1757)
The son of the prolific Italian composer Alessandro Scarlatti, Domenico was a musical genius. He left Italy in his early thirties to take a position at the court of Portugal where, as harpsichord teacher to the Infanta Maria Barbara, he began to develop his own style. Scarlatti took an interest in short forms. His sonatas are entirely original. Their AB form is the precursor to the sonata-allegro form. His single two-part movements consist of a modulation from home to a related key and the return. This piece is written in B minor.

Sonata *(K.25, L.481),* by Domenico Scarlatti (1685-1757)
Scarlatti's sonatas are tuneful and vivacious. His *galant,* sensitive style differs from the traditional Baroque, and must have been pleasing to his royal pupil, whom he followed from Portugal to Madrid when she married the heir to the Spanish throne. Scarlatti's sonatas are ingenious keyboard pieces, in which each note is of supreme importance. They often have contrasting themes, and the mood may vary from the lighthearted and comic to the dramatic and intense. This sonata is written in F sharp minor.

Prelude and Fugue No. 2 *(BWV 847),* by Johann Sebastian Bach (1685-1750)
Bach was born in Eisenach, Germany. Orphaned at an early age, he undertook the study of all the musical genres and instruments of his day, and taught himself composition by copying music. At the age of twenty, he traveled to hear the great organist and composer Buxtehude, who had a profound effect on his music. Little of Bach's music was published during his lifetime. While fellow musicians like Beethoven knew of his greatness, it was not until the 19th century, through the efforts of music historians as well as the composer Felix Mendelsshohn, that Bach was re-discovered, his manuscripts tracked down, and his compositions introduced to a grateful world.

Prelude and Fugue No. 9 *(BWV 854),* by Johann Sebastian Bach (1685-1750)
Bach's extraordinary skill at composition is demonstrated in part by the wide range of forms of music in which he was not only a master, but an innovator. A *fugue* is a musical flight of fancy (from the Italian word *fugue* for "flight"). It is a work of counterpoint in which a subject voice is answered in approximate imitation by at least two additional voices. The successive entries transpose the subject rather than echo it, providing freedom for innovation in harmony and development. For composers of the Baroque, the form allowed for the pairing of great contrapuntal skill and discipline with ornamentation and imagination. Bach's brilliance as a composer of the fugue has been unsurpassed, and the form reached its high point in his keyboard works. In the court at Cöthen, Bach composed the first book of *The Well-Tempered Clavier,* which contains forty-eight preludes and fugues.

Air with Variations, by George Frideric Handel (1685-1759)
Handel was born at Halle in Saxony. He played second violin in an orchestra there before traveling to Italy, where he met the leading figures of music, including Corelli and the Scarlattis. He mastered the Italian style in opera, chamber, and vocal music. After meeting success with an opera in London he settled there, eventually earning a lifetime pension from Queen Anne. George Frideric Handel composed operas, oratorios, concertos, cantatas, suites, and instrumental music. He contributed to every musical genre current in his time, both vocal and instrumental. Beethoven considered him the greatest composer who ever lived. *Air with Variations,* which is also known as *The Harmonious Blacksmith,* is from Handel's *Suite No. 5 in E minor.*

CLASSICAL ERA

Sonata in F major *(No. 38, Hob. XVI/33),* by Franz Joseph Haydn (1732-1809)
Haydn was born in Rohrau in Lower Austria. Though Franz was one of his names neither he nor his contemporaries ever used it; he was known as either Joseph or just Haydn. He was extremely prolific and had become the most celebrated composer of his time. Since the early 19th century he has been revered as the first of the three "Viennese Classics"–Haydn, Mozart, and Beethoven. He is most commonly known as the "Father of the Symphony" because of his important contributions to this form of music. Around 1761, Haydn started working for the noble Esterházy family, which was the richest and most influential family in Hungary, and it was during this period of employment that he composed the *Sonata in F major.*

Sonata in C minor *(Sonata Pathétique, Opus 13, First and Second Movements),*
by Ludwig van Beethoven (1770-1827)
Beethoven was born in Bonn, in the German Rhineland. As an adult he lived in Vienna, and while he never had a court appointment, he had patrons in an appreciative Viennese aristocracy, and earned income from publishing and performing. As a young man he suffered great despair after learning he had an affliction which eventually destroyed his hearing. His desire to produce his musical ideas saved his life, and he became the architect of the 19th century heroic vision of life. Beethoven believed that art could elevate experiences, and that if his listeners understood his music, they might be freed from some of the miseries of human life. In the *Sonata in C minor – Pathétique* – the emotional storms of the first movement are followed by sounds of consolation in the second. Beethoven's music expressed the rising democratic ideals of his time, which took written form in the American *Bill of Rights* of 1792.

Sonata in D major *(No. 50, Hob. XVI/37, First Movement),* by Franz Joseph Haydn (1732-1809)
There was no tradition of music in Haydn's family. He had a gift for singing and became a chorister at St. Stephen's Cathedral in Vienna at the age of eight. He was employed in 1761 on the estate of Prince Esterházy in western Hungary, and remained in full employment with this wealthy family until 1790. The Classical form of the sonata was simple, with two sections which were repeated. The Baroque era was one of innovation, and in Haydn's sonatas one can observe how the form was expanded. Essential features of the evolving form also appear in the works of Mozart and Beethoven.

Rondo alla Turca (from *Sonata in A major, KV 331, Third Movement),*
by Wolfgang Amadeus Mozart (1756-1791)
Mozart and Franz Joseph Haydn met in 1781 or 1782. In each other, they encountered skill and talent equal to their own, and they formed a deep friendship. Although Haydn was twenty five years Mozart's senior, he outlived him. Mozart was positively influenced by Haydn's innovations in form. It was Haydn who first developed the ingenious combination of rondo and sonata forms that Mozart joined so elegantly. His many sonatas provided enjoyment for his family, valuable teaching tools in his work with his students, and continually fresh material for intimate concerts of solo and chamber works for music-loving patrons, friends, and acquaintances. Mozart's *Sonata in A major* was composed in Munich or Vienna, between 1781 and 1783.

Sonata in B flat major *(KV 570, First Movement),* by Wolfgang Amadeus Mozart (1756-1791)
As the children of musician Leopold Mozart, Wolfgang Amadeus and his sister Nannerl were launched early into musical careers, performing at various European concerts and charming their audiences. Wolfgang was exceptionally precocious, and his musical brilliance such that it is said of him, "Mozart is music." His refined style met the needs of the aristocracy. His music is an assimilation of Italian, German and French influences. As an adult, Mozart preferred small, private performances among friends to large public concerts. His father Leopold once wrote to Nannerl that at a quartet party at Mozart's home, Haydn had remarked to him, "Before God… I tell you that your son is the greatest composer known to me… in person or by name." Mozart composed his Sonata in B flat major in Vienna in February of 1789.

ROMANTIC ERA

Dreaming *(Tu me parles du fond d'un rêve, Opus 15, No. 3),* by Amy Marcy Cheney Beach (1867-1944)
This American composer, a contemporary of Clara Schumann (1819-1896), was the most prominent woman composer of her time. As a child, Amy Marcy Cheney was a musical and intellectual prodigy. She hummed harmony to the lullabies her mother sang to her, learned to read books at the age of three, and played the piano and composed at four. Amy was born into a culture of American Puritanism, which held that performing was degrading for women. Nonetheless, she pursued her love of piano, and made her concert debut in 1883 at the age of sixteen with the Boston Symphony Orchestra. At eighteen she married, and retired from performing, while continuing to compose under the name "Mrs. H.H.A. Beach." Amy Beach believed that American artists should compose in the folk style of their own heritage, which for her was Scottish and Irish. In 1892, after hearing Antonin Dvořák's *New World Symphony,* she composed her magnificent *Gaelic Symphony,* the first important symphony by an American composer.

Intermezzo *(Opus 118, No. 2),* by Johannes Brahms (1833-1897)
Brahms began his career as a pianist, and composed and performed with great success in Hamburg, Germany. He moved to Vienna in 1862, where he achieved worldwide acclaim. In his first fifteen years there he did not publish any works for piano, concentrating instead on vocal, instrumental, and chamber music. Brahms is known primarily for his symphonies and concertos, but his songs and short piano pieces show him to be a master of lyricism. His piano repertoire includes *rhapsodies, fantasias, intermezzos, capriccios, romances,* and *ballades.* This work, Opus 118, consists of six *Clavierstücke* (piano pieces)—four *intermezzos,* a *ballade,* and a *romance.* They were published in 1893 and first performed in London in 1894.

Nocturne *(Opus 9, No. 1),* by Frédéric Chopin (1810-1849)
Frédéric François Chopin was born in Poland. His father was a French schoolteacher, and his mother a Polish woman of culture and refinement. The family lived in Warsaw. As a boy Chopin took piano lessons and studied the works of Bach, Haydn, Mozart, and Beethoven, and composed piano music with the titles *mazurkas, polonaises,* and *waltzes.* He gave his first public recital at the age of eight. On a journey to Paris at the age of twenty one, Chopin learned that the Russians had taken possession of his native Warsaw. Although Paris became his adoptive home, he is the national composer of Poland, and in his music there lies the reflection of his love for his homeland. The piano was Chopin's favorite instrument, and he wrote his highly innovative, distinctive, and very beautiful works almost exclusively for piano. His *nocturnes* (night songs) are tender, and tinged with melancholy. Chopin dedicated his three *Nocturnes Op. 9* to Marie Denise Pleyel (1811-1875), French pianist, teacher, composer, and wife of Camille Pleyel.

Consolation No. 5, by Franz Liszt (1811-1886)
The Hungarian composer and pianist Franz Liszt was the son of an official on the Esterházy estates. His father was a cellist in the court orchestra under both Haydn and Beethoven. Franz studied under Carl Czerny. As a student in Paris, he embraced French romanticism and the concept of the artist as prophet and priest. He became friends with the leading artists and intellectuals of the day: Heine, Balzac, Chopin, Berlioz, and Hugo, to name but a few. Liszt's many piano compositions include *études* and *fantasias*, character pieces, songs, sacred music, and a sonata. His concert works include symphonic poems, symphonies, concertos, and oratorios. He wrote keyboard versions of operas and of Beethoven's nine symphonies and in his *Hungarian Rhapsodies* he sought to recreate on the piano the sound and style of Gypsy orchestras.

Mazurka in A flat major *(Opus 59, No. 2)*, by Frédéric Chopin (1810-1849)
In Paris, Chopin was surrounded by the leading intellectuals of the day. He quickly established himself as a performer and teacher among the members of high society. The admiring musicians in his circle included Liszt, Berlioz, and Rossini. Heinrich Heine and the painter Delacroix were among his friends. In 1837 Liszt introduced him to Mme. Aurore Dudevant, famous under the nom de plume (pen name) George Sand, and they had an important relationship for eight years. She wrote of him that his "creative power was ... miraculous." Chopin is known as the "Poet of the Piano." He told his students that the piano "must be made to sing." His music ranges from powerful to delicate, with trills, grace notes, and light runs. His mazurkas are derived from a Polish peasant dance.

Wedding Day at Troldhaugen (from *Lyric Pieces, Opus 65, No. 6)*, by Edvard Grieg (1843-1907)
Edvard Grieg grew up in a middle-class family in Norway. His parents sent him to the Leipzig Conservatory, where he developed a love for the lyrical music of Robert Schumann. Grieg was introduced to Norwegian peasant culture by the Norwegian violinist Ole Bull. Grieg composed many sets of *Lyric Pieces (Lyrische Stücke)*, depicting elements of Norwegian life - scenes in the villages, in the countryside, in the forests, and at sea, folk events, and the color and emotion of Norwegian stories and lore. *Bryllupsdag på Troldhaugen* ("Wedding Day at Troldhaugen") is number six in an 1896 set. Grieg's genius lay in the songs and piano miniatures he composed evoking the Norwegian spirit - a haunting sense of loneliness combined with a mystical communion with nature.

20TH/21ST CENTURIES

Prelude in C sharp minor *(Opus 3, No. 2)*, by Sergei Rachmaninov (1873-1943)
Sergei Rachmaninov was born into a piano-playing family. He began his musical studies at the St. Petersburg Conservatory at the age of nine. By the time he was a teenager he had won the Moscow Conservatory's gold medal for an opera, and composed songs, a piano concerto, and the well-received, popular *Prelude in C sharp minor.* Rachmaninov's technique allowed him to draw sounds of great strength from the keyboard, and his writing, while lyrical and tender, is grand and soaring. He composed a symphonic poem, piano concertos, a choral symphony inspired by Edgar Allan Poe, and the lovely *All-Night Vigil* for an *a cappella* chorus. Rachmaninov left Russia after the Revolution of 1905 and became a touring pianist. He died in Beverly Hills, weeks after becoming an American citizen.

Poem No. 1 (from *2 Poèmes, Opus 32),* by Alexander Nikolayevich Scriabin (1872-1915)
The Russian composer Alexander Scriabin was a contemporary of Sergei Rachmaninov, although Rachmaninov outlived him by some thirty years. Scriabin's mother was one of Russia's first female musicians to gain recognition. When she died within a year of her son's birth, a loving aunt took responsibility for him. In her care he played the piano, wrote plays, created needlework and toy pianos, and read English and French literature. Like other Russians in the era before the Revolution in 1905, Scriabin considered art a superior form of knowledge revealing the transcendent and divine. He had a vast intellect, and was attracted to mysticism. He discussed color and music with Rachmaninov and Rimsky-Korsakov, and assigned colors to keys.

Capriccio (from *Pièces Brèves, Opus 84, No. 1),* by Gabriel Fauré (1845-1924)
Gabriel Fauré was a French composer, teacher, pianist, and organist whose many accomplishments influenced the course of French music. He is widely regarded as the greatest master of French song. He studied for eleven years at the Ecole Niedermeyer in Paris where his first compositions were songs set to verses by Victor Hugo. He was awarded literary prizes as well as musical prizes for *solfège* (sight-singing), harmony, and piano. Fauré's charming and elegant first works for piano made him famous. They show the influence of Chopin, Saint-Saëns, and Liszt. Fauré was a teacher of great influence at the Paris Conservatory. His impeccable taste left its mark on every genre in which he worked.

Romance *(Opus 24, No. 9),* by Jean Sibelius (1865-1957)
Jean Sibelius was born in a Russian garrison town in Finland to a Swedish-speaking family. The country had been under the political control of Sweden for 800 years before Russia took it over in the 19th century. Sibelius was educated in his country's first Finnish-speaking grammar school, where he became acquainted with Finnish mythology. As a student in Germany and Vienna, Austria, he steeped himself in Finnish culture. As Finnish dreams of self-determination began to stir in the 19th century, Sibelius forged a Finnish national music. In his orchestral works he masterfully conveyed the grandeurs and mysteries of Finland's folk myths and natural landscapes. Finland won her independence from Russia in 1917. Sibelius completed his *Romance No. 9 in D flat minor* in 1901.

Etude de Sonorité No. 1, by François Morel (1926-)
The Canadian composer François d'Assise Morel studied at the Conservatory of Music in Montreal, remaining there to pursue a career in composition. His reach as a musician was wide. He composed incidental music and popular songs for the Canadian Broadcasting Corporation. He founded an association for the promotion of contemporary music, as well as an ensemble for wood and wind instruments. He composed symphonies for jazz band and for small orchestras; works for solo instruments—piano, flute, organ, guitar, clarinet, and cello; works for string quartets and quintets; songs and études. His two *Etudes de sonorité* ("studies in resonance," or "sound") were written for the piano in 1954.

Clair de lune (from *Suite bergamasque),* by Claude Debussy (1862-1918)
Claude Debussy's ancestors were of the French peasantry. His parents kept a china shop. Debussy loved music, and entered the Paris Conservatory when he was eleven, where his harmonic innovations were unsettling to his teachers. In time they came to have a profound effect on the art of composition. Debussy participated in artistic circles where his contact with artists and writers led him to conclude that scents, colors, and sounds correspond

to one another. He wrote masterful, short mood pieces with such impressionist titles as *The Snow Is Dancing.* He established the independence of the French song from the German lied. Among his best-known works are the *Suite bergamesque,* a four movement work for piano containing the famous Claire de lune ("Moonlight") and his 1876 tone poem *Prélude à l'Après-Midi d'un faune.*

The Cat and the Mouse *(Scherzo Humoristique),* by Aaron Copland (1900-1990)
Aaron Copland was born in Brooklyn, New York to Russian Jewish immigrants. During his twenties he studied in Paris. Copland believed that music should be personal and portray disciplined emotion rather than mere technique. In 1936 Copland composed a popular orchestral piece based on Mexican melodies and rhythms. His three popular ballets *Billy the Kid, Rodeo,* and *Appalachian Spring* soon followed. He wrote two works for high school students and the scores for many films, among them *Of Mice and Men, Our Town, The Red Pony,* and *The Heiress,* for which he won an Academy award. His *Twelve Poems of Emily Dickinson* was written for voice and piano. Another important, quintessentially American piece was *A Lincoln Portrait* for speaker and chorus, based on text from Abraham Lincoln's speeches.

Rialto Ripples *(Rag),* by George Gershwin (1898-1937) and Will Donaldson (1891-1954)
As a young man George Gershwin's two-fold aspiration was to bring the fullest capacities of concert music to popular song, and to carry the idioms of popular American music—ragtime, blues, and the ballad—into serious compositions. Gershwin debuted as a serious composer in 1924, with the world premiere of his *Rhapsody in Blue* at a concert of American music in New York City; the work received a standing ovation. In collaboration with his brother Ira as lyricist, George Gershwin wrote many cherished American works, among them *Porgy and Bess, Swanee, I Got Rhythm, The Man I Love, But Not For Me,* and *Lady, Be Good!* He wrote songs for musicals and films, works for orchestra and string quartet, and works for piano that included preludes and waltzes. Gershwin's *An American in Paris* is an early example of the use of nonmusical sounds (i.e., Parisian taxihorns) for serious artistic purposes. *Rialto Ripples* is a rag, composed with the American musician Will Donaldson around 1916.

Minuet on the Name of Haydn *(Menuet sur le nom d'Haydn),* by Maurice Ravel (1875-1937)
The French composer Maurice Ravel was an impressionist/post-impressionist. He studied composition at the Paris Conservatory under the great teacher Gabriel Fauré. He was inspired by his association with the avant-garde poets, painters, and musicians of Paris. Respected in innovative circles, he was at first rejected by critics. Like Claude Debussy, Ravel exemplified the Gallic spirit. He had a classical streak, an affinity for nature, a love of dance rhythms, and a gift for putting the French language to music. His work was refined. He believed that the purpose of art was to please the senses. His orchestral works won international acclaim.

Bulgarian Dance No. 2 (from *Six Dances in Bulgarian Rhythm),* by Béla Bartók (1881-1945)
Béla Bartók was a Hungarian composer, pianist, and ethnomusicologist. His parents were keen amateur musicians. He studied at the Budapest Academy of Music, where he was a student of István Thomán, one of Franz Liszt's most gifted pupils. Bartók earned his living from teaching and playing the piano, but he was a relentless collector of peasant songs from local villages. He collaborated with fellow Hungarian composer and ethnomusicologist Zoltán Kodály on a volume of 150 Transylvanian songs. He prepared an edition of 3,000 Slovak folk songs, and wrote an extensive study of Romanian *colinde* (Christmas songs). He published articles on folk song and on 20th century music. He wrote music for the stage, orchestra, and chorus; chamber and piano music; and many songs. His short pieces include many mazurkas, polkas and Ländler.